Levinas, Ethics and Law

Levinas, Ethics and Law

Matthew Stone

EDINBURGH
University Press

Edinburgh University Press is one of the leading university presses
in the UK. We publish academic books and journals in our selected
subject areas across the humanities and social sciences, combining
cutting-edge scholarship with high editorial and production values to
produce academic works of lasting importance. For more information
visit our website: edinburghuniversitypress.com

Edinburgh University Press Ltd
The Tun – Holyrood Road
12 (2f) Jackson's Entry
Edinburgh EH8 8PJ

First published in hardback by Edinburgh University Press 2016

Typeset in 11/13 Goudy Old Style by
Servis Filmsetting Ltd, Stockport, Cheshire,
and printed and bound in Great Britain by
CPI Group (UK) Ltd, Croydon CR0 4YY

A CIP record for this book is available from the British Library

ISBN 978 1 4744 0076 3 (hardback)
ISBN 978 1 4744 3254 2 (paperback)
ISBN 978 1 4744 0077 0 (webready PDF)
ISBN 978 1 4744 1514 9 (epub)

Contents

Acknowledgements

Many people other than me bear responsibility for this book coming into being, but perhaps none more than Costas Douzinas, under whom I studied for my PhD some years ago. My initial interest in Levinas, and some of the ideas that would eventually lead to the writing of this book, are products of working with Costas. I can only offer pale imitations of the philosophical wisdom and political commitment that he embodies and from which I have learnt so much.

I would also like to thank other friends who helped shape my thinking along the way. I cannot provide an exhaustive list, so I will pick out just a few names. Illan rua Wall, Victoria Ridler and Gilbert Leung have all had an immeasurable influence that permeates the arguments I present here.

I am grateful to the School of Law at the University of Essex, where the eventual research and writing took place, some of which whilst I was on research leave.

It has been a pleasure to work with John Watson and Ellie Bush at Edinburgh University Press, who have both provided support, guidance and patience in appropriate measure. Especial thanks go also to the anonymous readers of the book proposal and the manuscript, whose careful and incisive comments were extremely valuable, and to Sarah Burnett for her invaluable editorial work.

Even when writing on my own, I was never on my own. Thank you Victoria.

Part I
The Importance of Ethics

I

Introduction: The Law's Other

The truest violence of law is not attributable to its errors, but to its essence. As a structure of meaning and a source of norms, framed through general and abstract standards, law has an especial, inevitable capacity to misrecognise 'the other' at the precise moment that the other is in most need of its justice. The significance of the other, upon which Levinas speaks with unparalleled philosophical authority, is instead personal, unique, singular, and fundamental in informing our understanding of ourselves, our desires and our duties. This book addresses law's difficult task of responding meaningfully to the type of ethical provocation that Levinas argues the other delivers. It is also about how his theory of ethics can allow us to challenge our own conceptions of law and, more importantly, how the complex relation between law and the other helps us understand what makes us human.

First, it is worth asking why we would want to think about this connection between law and human subjectivity. For many, law might well appear merely as a system of rules and punishment. Such a definition, exemplified by the early English legal positivists, allows us to limit our relationship with law to the injunction not to disobey. Command theory, associated indelibly with Jeremy Bentham and John Austin, famously held that law ought to be defined as a code of behavioural imperatives issued by a legitimated authority and backed by the threat of punishment. It is little coincidence that the jurisprudence of nineteenth-century Britain, which was emerging as a global economic powerhouse, would pander to the idea that law only really addresses wrongdoers, and that the compliant, industrious majority can freely get along fine without worrying too much about what it has to say. A central premise – perhaps even a presumption – of this book is that the law does not simply regulate our behaviour, but also plays a fundamental role in determining our senses of ourselves. This book adopts a much wider notion of the 'legal subject' than the common one, described exemplarily by another totemic figure of orthodox jurisprudence, Hans Kelsen, as simply 'he who is the subject of a legal obligation or of a right'.[1] Beyond abstract entitlements and duties, beyond statute books and law reports, beyond the grandiose architecture of courts and Parliament, beyond prisons and parole officers, the law plays a fundamental role in building us as subjects, from bottom-up. The way we interpret the world and think of ourselves and others is always processed through thick legal filters. It is true to say that we are 'legal subjects', but not merely in the sense that we are 'subjected' to the laws of the state as Kelsen would have it, not merely in the way that we have an abstract existence as legal entities, but also in the way that our basic mode of being, living and thinking is conditioned by a legal matrix of norms and knowledge. In other words, we are not simply subjects that must abide by legal rules; we are *subjectified*, produced as subjects, by law. Such a claim of course relies upon a number of theoretical premises, which can be initially summed up neatly with reference to Drucilla Cornell, who wrote that, 'law is embedded in ontology, in a shared social reality'.[2] By referring, quite rightly, to 'ontology' Cornell evokes the way in which law does not simply teach codes of behaviour, to which we can take a critical and interpretive distance. As ontology, law authors our understanding of being itself, both our being as subjects, and the being of the world around us. Of course, law cannot subsume all aspects of subjectivity. There must be elements of our experience that exceed – even rupture – the understanding of existence that law grants to us. But what Levinas helps expose in this regard is not a plurality of ways of understanding being, but instead, that which eludes ontology altogether. That which is truly *other*. It is in this gap that we have the opportunity to inquire into our relation with the law more critically, thinking about the limits and failures of law in its governance of life, and how our subjectivity may be constructed in critique of or even resistance to the law. The extent to which our subjectivity reaches out beyond a legalised understanding of the world, or a 'legal ontology', and specifically in the way that this gesture operates in a response to radical otherness, is the structure of ethics that this book traces in the work of Levinas.

The Persistence of the Other

The backdrop of this book is a critical review of the current reception of Levinas's ideas into legal and political theory. To provide some initial context, a few words can be said here by way of a brief biography. At the time of his death in 1995, Levinas had become renowned for his critical interpretation of the presumptions of Western philosophy, and for his defence of subjectivity, which, he argued, is constituted by an 'ethical', unconditionally responsible relation to alterity. Having grown up in his native Lithuania, a formative early episode in the development of these ideas was his attendance of the University of Freiberg in 1928, where he would study under Edmund Husserl. It was also here that he was introduced to the work of Martin Heidegger, towards whom he showed great enthusiasm up until the latter's joining of the Nazi Party. Much of his mature work came to resemble a critique of the priority of being reflected in Heidegger's philosophy and its legacy. Levinas would later spend time during the war imprisoned in Fallingbostel labour camp, during which he wrote what would eventually become published as *Existence and Existents*, a stunningly poetic work that meditates, perhaps tellingly, on themes such as solitude and the desire to transcend the enchainment to oneself. But it was not until 1961 that he published his first masterwork, *Totality and Infinity: An Essay on Exteriority*, a complex and evocative meditation on all aspects of the impression made upon human life by the encounter with alterity. After this book eventually received wide attention (notably by that ubiquitous figure of the contemporary French academy, Jacques Derrida), he published a further major work of philosophy, the more focused and thematically bleaker *Otherwise than Being or Beyond Essence*, in 1974. Since then, his ideas have been gradually received by many disciplines in addition to philosophy, including of course law.

Yet Levinas himself wrote relatively little directly on the subject of law, which might be especially surprising given the breadth of scope of some of his works. Nevertheless, he has had notable influence in critical and interdisciplinary legal studies, this sometimes being acknowledged with a hint of scepticism.[3] Whether an adoption of Levinasian ideas in legal theory, if it really exists, might form part of a wider phenomenon dubbed by Fred Alford as the 'Levinas effect', is open to debate. This, Alford says, is 'the ability of Levinas's texts to say anything the reader wants to hear, so that Levinas becomes a deconstructionist, postmodern, or protofeminist, even the reconciler of postmodern ethics and rabbinic Judaism'.[4] The philosopher Simon Critchley similarly warned that Levinas's explosive influence on 'religious studies and theology, sociology, aesthetics, literary, and cultural theory, and even...political theory' has led to a burgeoning of 'exegesis, commentary, comparison with other thinkers, and, at its worst, homage.'[5] This book therefore hopes to proceed in a way that is mindful of the evident concerns about instrumentalising Levinas's work, whilst at the same time recognising the necessity of putting Levinas into dialogue with other critical apparatuses for understanding law.

Levinas's work is not always easy to interpret, nor even, on occasion, to fully understand. Even at its most poetic it can be abstruse and intensely difficult to read, and slow to reward even the most tenacious. It often presumes, typically on an unspoken basis, a working knowledge of other continental thinkers. It can sometimes be a gruelling – and ultimately fruitless – effort to trace a linear analytic structure in his arguments (*Otherwise than Being*, in particular, is written in a dizzying pattern where concepts are frequently utilised before they are explained fully). Yet somehow, as evidenced by the 'Levinas effect', there is an enduring and widely felt sense that Levinas explicated something intuitive about our senses of ourselves and of our responsibility to others, our private identities and our relationship with authority.

Much of human endeavour is structured by an attempt to grasp and absorb. The post-Enlightenment dominance of the human as the emancipatory figure of rational enterprise ought to have guaranteed our sanity and our mutual protection. Instead, as we look back over the previous century (a century that Levinas saw almost in its entirety) we are left with abundant images of madness and death. A century whose pivot, at least for the West, was Auschwitz. It may well be the case that the resonance of Levinas's work lies in the way he traces the very limits of our rationalist conquest, whilst avoiding the nihilist excesses of certain fervent postmodernisms. Whilst the letter of his philosophy is often decidedly abstract, a fair appreciation of Levinas's intellectual oeuvre should not seek to isolate his ideas from the political context of his own life.[6] It is little coincidence that his work would repeatedly return to the way that our peculiar relations with others offer a horizon of escape, of freedom from both solitude and authority. For all of our knowledge, our capacity to represent, to translate and assimilate, there is always a certain enigma about our emplacement with others that escapes the domain of the sciences. Within this enigma, certain practices that one might judge to be 'mad', persecutory obsessions, unconditional duties to strangers, the discontinuity of time, are found to be basic components of how to live.

Levinas's work springs out of a critique of ontology, that is, the idea that to philosophise is to understand our relation with being. For Levinas, being expresses, or tends towards the expression of, totality. It deems to articulate everything. For Levinas, the encounter with the other person expresses something that escapes totality, something that is otherwise than being. This radical form of signification, which for Levinas is

pre-ontological, has the capacity to level a direct and singular provocation, an ethical challenge, to the subject that experiences it, one that
calls into question the most basic elements of the subject's ontological
grasp on reality: its autonomy, its freedom. His work elucidates a schism
between ontology and ethics, and as one can immediately anticipate, the
challenge posed to law by Levinas's work is as necessary as it is difficult.
Laws are general and universal; legal judgment has a capacity to assert a
factual knowledge of events and a juridical determination of their culpability. Yet law is always called upon to try to comprehend real, unique
events: human encounters whose otherness has the power to slip through
the law's ontology. Whether the law assimilates otherness, or whether it
responds ethically (indeed, whether it is even possible to respond ethically) is Levinas's ultimate question for law, and is a question rooted in
a wider concern for justice. The remainder of this chapter, whilst reserv-
ing substantial engagement with Levinas's philosophy for the next, will
explore a few thematic threads which allow us to frame the importance
and difficulty of the question of the other for law.

Ethics, Morality and Orthodox Jurisprudence

It is fair, although simplistic, to say that Levinasian ethics are concerned
with how we respond to those who are different to us. It is hopefully
useful, therefore, to first indicate the way in which Levinas understood
the nature of difference, and moreover how it is distinct from the sort of
conceptual framework used in more familiar sources of legal and political
philosophy. In order to do so, Levinas's idiosyncratic approach to ethics
will be contrasted briefly with the ways that Anglo-American theory
tends to frame difference through plural moral outlooks.

Given that anyone who has already studied jurisprudence will be
familiar, perhaps painfully so, with the debate between the legal positivist
H. L. A. Hart and Lord Patrick Devlin in the late 1950s and 1960s,[7] this
is perhaps an appropriately recognisable place to start. In these theorists'
writings, morality is understood as a set of substantive values, typically
those held by a social majority. The key question is what legitimacy the
law has in enforcing such morals. The wider picture that is painted by this
debate is between a positivist outlook that regards law as a formal system
of legitimated rules, represented by Hart, and an attempted revival of the
position that law must contain an intrinsic set of natural moral values,
championed by Devlin. Taking a step back further still, one is presented
with an overtly political debate. On the one hand, we find arguments in
favour of the liberal state allowing for a plurality of changeable values to

be articulated and protected, and on the other, a much more conservative model of substantive morals being sustained via the machinery of
governance.

As Devlin's moral essentialism was accompanied by an indefensible
objection to the legalisation of sex between men, it is of little surprise
that the liberal side of this debate won. The central positions of Anglo-
American jurisprudence are largely tied to the political philosophy of
liberalism, positing law as a structure of common agreement which can
regulate people's own pursuits of their differing desires and values. But
whilst for Hart the validity of law is not dependent upon its articulation
of any particular moral outlook, there are two important ways in which
values emerge in his theory. The first is that in order for law to function it
must protect some fundamental values, such as the value of human life.[8]
The second is much more crucial however, and is revealed in the centrality of a natural right to equal freedom that Hart attributes to his conception of legality.[9] Once this is accepted, Hart's argument can proceed in
broad adherence to the liberalism of John Stuart Mill: interference with
this freedom must be justified to be legitimate, and the principle means
of justification is to show that the interference is necessary to prevent
harm.[10] When the law encounters the other, it ought to allow the other
sufficient freedom to realise itself within a pluralistic society, except where
it poses some form of threat.

When posed alongside Devlin's caricature of social conservatism,
Hart's position seems eminently reasonable. However, it fails to negotiate
the problem that dogs any liberal theory of law, which is how one can
posit a framework for the pluralism of values that is not itself predicated
on a value at its origin. In order to facilitate a pluralistic diversity of
interests, jurisprudence must inevitably give expression to a wider and
determinate set of moral ideas. For example, the moral priority of the
individual, the centrality of rights, and the function of the market as a
means of structuring society are all implicit values reflected in the very
foundation of liberal governance. The extent to which radically divergent
alternative ideas about political community can be accommodated within
such a framework is therefore inescapably limited. Furthermore, as will be
covered towards the end of the book, by promoting a formalistic protection of plurality the substantive content of such principles has the effect
of appearing apolitically normal and natural. Alternative conceptions of
social life thereby risk contortion in the way they are interpreted.

Furthermore, Hart encounters difficulties when claiming that the
authority of legal principles derives from a structure of legal reason-

ing, unfettered by the brutish power of the state. Hart famously posits the existence of a 'rule of recognition' capable of identifying valid law, which is necessary for the coherence of any modern legal system. As Peter Fitzpatrick has noted adeptly, by having to identify the apex of English law's legitimacy as simply 'whatever the Queen in parliament enacts as law' Hart can resort to little more than legal faith when the conceptual integrity of parliamentary supremacy is interrogated.[11] Whilst Hart's jurisprudence attempts to disarm law by claiming that it is authorised by a coherent and acceptable internal logic, he is never able to fully depart from the nexus between legitimacy and sheer power. Once our understanding of the apparatus of sovereign power is renewed as the ultimate source of law's authority, the problematic of how law recognises and responds to its other is redoubled in intensity and complexity.

Continuing with the theme of liberal theory's approach to accommodating difference, Rawls's *A Theory of Justice*, another iconic text of legal theory syllabi, encounters the same problem in a more pronounced manner. Rawls is interested in identifying the basic principles of a just legal system. The principles he identifies are a commitment to constitutional rights and distributive justice, which are arrived at by working through what mutually disinterested parties would choose if detached from their lived reality and forced to devise the social structure they would then enter. The power of Rawls's theoretical position is in its neo-Kantian methodology, arguing that the specific rights of people and redistributive powers of the state result from an impartial position of rational consensus. Again, the task of liberal jurisprudence is to claim that its structures transcend matters of personal value, and provide a platform upon which we can all agreeably co-exist. Of course, the idea that a group of people who are not already committed to liberal principles would prioritise individualistic rights is problematic, and this criticism of Rawls is well documented.[12] In his later work *Political Liberalism*, Rawls shifted the terms of his theory away from a moral position based on abstracted rationality, and towards an overtly political theory. The book opens by taking as granted the 'fact of reasonable pluralism', and poses the idea of society as 'a system of fair cooperation and that its fair terms be reasonable to all to accept is part of its idea of reciprocity'.[13] By relying on themes such as society's overlapping consensus and practices of public reason, Rawls is interested in the ways his idea of justice can manifest in a fairly narrow, yet entirely conventional, political culture that presumes from the outset a foundation of social agreement. In a similar way, Ronald Dworkin's jurisprudence pursues a liberalism rooted in a general entitlement to equal

concern and respect. He argues that there is a privileged mode of legal reasoning that extends beyond the technical application of discrete rules and
into broader matters of principle, and which allows for the community to
express itself in the assertion of law as a coherent, seamless whole. When
Dworkin writes that a 'community of principle accepts integrity',[14] he
means that where a society orients itself around a mutually agreeable set
of principles, it is necessary for them to be able to reason with that matrix
of principles as an unbroken totality. By interpreting and reinterpreting
that web of principles in real, lived scenarios, law achieves its legitimacy.
Again, we encounter the problem of how the law can respond, meaningfully and ethically, to those others who lie outside the consensus of a
social majority, and beyond the totality of principles upon which legal
reasoning is predicated. In differing ways, each of these totemic figures of
legal theory negotiates a tension within liberal theory, between the need
for a platform upon which people can pursue differing moral convictions
on the one hand, and the need for such a platform to be generally acceptable across society on the other. What each of them arrives at is a form
of moderate moral pluralism, in which disparate conceptions of how we
live our lives can be accommodated only so long as we all subscribe to
roughly the same ideas about rights and justice. Not only do such outlooks
manifestly fail to provide a framework in which deep difference, radical
otherness, can be apprehended, they also relegate political differences to
the level of mere personal preference.

The limitations of such approaches are identified quite succinctly
when Chantal Mouffe, in her reading of Carl Schmitt, summarises that
'every consensus is based on acts of exclusion'.[15] Schmitt's concern with
liberalism was that it tends towards depoliticisation, by which differences
are sublated into a political machinery incapable of negotiating genuine
disparity.[16] If politics concerns collective identity, any assertion of consensus operates to the exclusion of inevitable and irreducible social antag-
onism. This is readily evident in the tension between Rawls's attempt
to posit a purely rational idea of liberal justice, and his concession that
this nevertheless presumes a politically partial set of preferences for freedom, the protection of the individual, and a reciprocal accommodation
of 'reasonable' differences. Even despite this concession, the terrain of
fundamental social disagreement, far from politicising the liberal society,
is instead pushed aside by it. Such is the political 'blind spot' of liberal
theory.[17] Levinas's insight in this area is, in the same vein, to illuminate
the deep-set fragility of any such totalising claim to rational consensus.
Whether Levinas must abandon or merely reconfigure the core tenets

of liberalism is a question taken up later. Certainly, he retained a commitment to the idea of the liberal state as a potential site through which the political risks of totality could be overcome. For conventional liberal theory, however, anything that exists outside of the terms of consensus has a tendency to take on a necessarily irrational, politically degenerate appearance, threatening the very terms upon which law and politics operate. As Michel Foucault has commented at length, this is the inevitable consequence of any regime of power that claims to be legitimated by the natural, rational (or indeed, 'reasonable') quality of its basic principles.[18] In such instances, genuine otherness can resultantly be dismissed as outside the concern of the central field of politics. One only has to consider the way in which recent US and UK military excursions, as well as those governments' simultaneous attacks on their populations' civil rights, were regularly justified either in the archaic language of extreme morality ('axis of evil', and so on) or the apolitical terminology of public safety.

It is suggested that the liberal approach to responding to social differences, which tends to be framed within the language of moral pluralism, fails to engage with the ethical challenge of real alterity. Whilst being opposed to an overt moral essentialism that sees the other as an active threat to the ethical life of community, moral pluralism nevertheless only allows for a diversity of values to be accommodated so long as they are expressed within a shared structure of principles. Levinas's concern with ethics transcends the debate over morality and law. His ethics are not a prescriptive code of moral behaviour, evocative of 'medical ethics' for instance. Nor are they a framework in which divergent moral opinions can be negotiated. Instead, his ethics concern the ways we respond and take responsibility for those who exceed our own universal viewpoint, and our own ontological way of comprehending the world around us. Levinas did not favour the idea that philosophy is rooted in a unifying conception of people's being, which he felt had been a feature of Western philosophy since Parmenides. Instead, he would emphasise the irreducible gap between people's being. The way in which we respond to this otherness, both in terms of appreciating the limits of cognition and knowledge, and the manner in which we interact with others, therefore becomes crucial. When we encounter someone that is different to us (in other words, any other person), the ethics of our response is not to purport to understand their difference, nor mount a weak pretence at pluralism by assimilating otherness into a shared platform for expressing differing personal preferences. Each inflicts a certain kind of ontological violence, whereby the other person's otherness is incorporated into one's own understanding of the world. The ethical challenge that Levinas describes is to endure a difficult process where one's own familiar understanding is undone. Ethical agency in Levinas is therefore unlike that of the moral subject in Kant, which is predicated on making the autonomous choice that stands as if it were universal law.[19] Rather, Levinas's ethics are based on the fracturing of autonomy, and the realisation that our understanding is not in itself enough to explain our ethical drives.

Law, Otherness and Madness

The essence of legal reasoning is authorisation and justification. What makes law *law* is that we can distinguish it from other norms by showing how it is grounded in legitimate authority. The poststructuralist movement argued that philosophy holds a comparable approach to its own sense of foundation. Treating philosophy as a literary endeavour, Derrida drew attention to the privileging of the spoken word as the articulation of an essential and present ground, of which all writing is a derivative representation. This can be called 'logocentricism'.[20] The centrality of law to certain logocentric projects allowed the critical legal scholars Douzinas, Warrington and McVeigh to coin the indulgent but wonderfully tongue-twisting neologism of 'logonomocentricism'. This, the authors explained, is 'the claim of the unity of self and others in absolute reason of the law'.[21] It denotes not merely the preoccupation with the presence of reason (*logos*), but also the coincidence of reason with law (*nomos*). The phenomenon of logonomocentricism therefore appears when the search for ground casts its gaze upon a specifically legal terrain.

In this way, the authors lead us to consider the textual and ontological violence of the law, which arises in the way that the fallacious appeal to unity between subjects, objects and laws inevitably produces an exclusionary effect upon others. In fact, there is a double violence here. On the one hand, one finds a familiar violence of a text whose inscription and interpretation is monopolised by an elite minority, and which has the material effect of legitimating physical force (imprisonment, fines, compulsion or prohibition to perform certain acts and, in some parts of the world, killing). But it is the second form of violence that is more of interest, and which arises out of the law's logonomocentric pretence. It is the violence of repudiating alterity; this being not merely a denial of the presence of the other within the law, but also a denial of its absence.

In the same way that the logocentric philosopher expresses a determined, fully present economy of meaning, the law, in its totality, appears always capable of giving an answer. Its rationality is always able to fully cognise a set of events and declare what is right and wrong, legal and unlawful. The rationality of law thus purports to be total; there is no 'other' that falls outside of its understanding. What is more, the solution purports to already be there, therefore avoiding the risks of retroactivity. If this proposition seems naive, it is worth remembering that it has enjoyed explicit support in the field of Anglo-American jurisprudence. To return to a figure mentioned earlier in this chapter, Ronald Dworkin (in)famously argued that legal argument is not so much a search for the best or most persuasive answer to a problem, but finding the *right* answer.[22] This position is predicated on a theory that holds legal reasoning to be a process of assembling and re-assembling principles into a coherent totality. If one accepts that such a seamless whole is logically possible (even if not actually existent), it follows that there must be a right way in which to solve any problem that arises. It may take time, it may be undermined by human error and it may be expensive, but if we pose an imaginary, incomparably perfect legal interpreter – named Hercules by Dworkin – then the law will always provide him with the applicable solution.[23]

It is easy to attack Dworkin for this relentlessly idealistic vision, but in an important sense he is right. Law *is* a fabric of meaning that purports to incorporate all phenomena into its understanding of the society it governs. Of course, it would be naïve to claim that law can operate as a true metaphysical totality; it can only be violently *asserted* as a totality (here we might lament Dworkin's obtuse and undeveloped dismissal of the critical insights of what he calls 'French linguistics').[24] Where difficult and unusual facts and problems look as though they may slip through its interstices, the law will always claim to weave them back in. The job of the critical Dworkinian, if such a figure exists, is to reveal that this Herculean process is profoundly violent and exclusionary, and the seamless web of meaning can be no more than a false claim to totality, meaning that every incorporation of life into law produces an excluded trace, or other. It is the process of assimilation, the ability to break up, categorise and interpret phenomena in accordance with a pre-existing bank of legal knowledge that allows the law to always offer an answer.

Curiously, Dworkin's choice of Hercules as the figurative ideal judge is quite apt. According to the famous Greek legend, this ancient mythical hero was commanded to perform twelve heroic labours by King Eurystheus. The story of the labours of Hercules is one of tenacity, commitment and courage, and the antithesis of apathy and indecision. Therefore he might persuasively resemble the perfect judge, unswayed by external pressures, determined to fulfil his duty to the Crown. Some might object that the figure of the judge Hercules can tell us little about the reality of law, given real-life judges' inconvenient proclivity for imperfection. Yet the myth may tell us more about the actual work of the judiciary than we might at first assume. Prior to his heroic adventures, Hercules was a capricious madman. Driven insane by Hera, the goddess of women and marriage, he slaughtered all six of his sons. His twelve labours, commissioned by Eurystheus only once he regained his sanity, were rites of atonement for this murder. There are two versions of Hercules therefore, one mad and one sane, but what remains consistent is his predilection for violence, whether in the senseless and unjust murder of his offspring, or in the sanctioned killing of fantastical beasts upon the authority of the sovereign. Surely it would be the latter version, the determined and repentant Hercules, who is needed in the work of law, and the science of deciding of hard cases? Yet we might be prompted to think otherwise by Derrida, who – in works informed pervasively by Levinasian ethics[25] – has written repeatedly on the way that madness is at the heart of all genuine decisions.[26] A decision that follows a predetermined rationality or formula is no decision, in that it is calculable, akin to solving an arithmetic problem. A decision only becomes possible when something is *undecidable*, in that the alternatives are of some kind of heterogenous species and so something foreign to the domain of rule and calculation must be introduced in order to arrive at one option to the dismissal of the other.[27] If we take Derrida's reflection seriously we find that, somewhat ironically, it is the insane Hercules who makes the true decision, the mad jump to one of several undecidable poles.

Derrida's own exemplar of such a decision is the story of the sacrifice of Isaac – which holds a conspicuous infanticidal parallel with the legend of Hercules. The narrative has it that God issued Abraham with a command to kill Isaac, his son. Far from claiming this to be exceptional, Derrida asks, 'isn't this also the most common thing?'[28] Isn't all responsibility based on an incalculable, and therefore unjustifiable, decision? Again, in an overtly Levinasian vein, Derrida posits that such a decision must transcend an immanent economy of knowledge. The question of whether a non-contradictory, seamless web of principles is logically possible is, ultimately, metaphysical, and depends entirely on how we characterise the nature of knowledge and ontology. For Derrida, language is a flux of identity and difference and has no privileged access to underlying presence, despite such access being a recurring presumption of the Western philosophical tradition.[29] Dworkin, reflecting an opposing logocentric outlook, avoids defending his claims to such an analysis of language and meaning, simply stating that the least sceptical position (his) should be preferred.[30]

A Levinasian position holds that for as long as there is the other person, there is the irreducible encounter with alterity; for as long as there is alterity, it is impossible to posit a total economy of knowledge without remainder. In turn, this is the condition of the (im)possibility of the decision. But if the condition of possibility of the decision is its impossibility, how do we arrive at a decision that is not arbitrary? In the eulogistic *Adieu to Emmanuel Levinas*, Derrida returns to the enigma of the decision, and whether it demands we conceive of it as always the decision '*of the other*'.[31] He was right to preface this claim by questioning whether Levinas himself would be comfortable with such a bold formulation. But he is similarly right in identifying Levinas as a thinker who, more than most others, could explain the emptiness and impossibility of a supposed decision that starts and ends with the egotic self. That a decision is undecidable does not entail that no meaningful decision can be made. It signals the manner in which heterogenous assignment, an irrevocable and involuntary affect of the other that forms the basis of Levinas's ethics, determines the decision on behalf of the subject.

It is in the idea of madness that one finds a link between Levinas's critique of humanism and the practices of law. To be affected by the other in the deep subjective sense that Levinas means is, for him, evocative of psychosis.[32] In other words, our singular and shattering relation with others is a form of detachment from the bourgeois familiarity of reality, a tear in the weave of ontology in which the strangeness of alterity ridicules the complacent homeliness of our world. Levinas would be correct in his use of this specifically medical term. In clinical contexts psychosis is associated with hallucinatory or delusional states in which patients lose their grasp on the objective world around them. In the more esoteric Lacanian canon of psychoanalysis, psychosis is thought of as a gap in the symbolic order caused by the absence of the legislative effect of paternal forbiddance.[33] Similarly for Levinas, psychosis is a moment of removal from the realm of onto-normative everydayness, and into an obsessive, persecutory encounter, the alterity of which opens radically new lines of possibility and of freedom. In this way, Levinas allows us to rethink the couplings of presence and absence, reason and madness, and justice and murder. The logocentric appeal to fill presence was capable of producing the perverted legality of the Nazis, and then the spiralling horrors of the death camps. Meanwhile, the 'psychosis' of ethics, a commitment to the other that transcends the fullness of being, is presented by Levinas as a fragile foundation of ethics and, ultimately, the question of justice.

A Note on 'Ethics' and Critical Legal Theory

It is important to understand that Levinas's ethics are unlike almost every other form of ethics. It is notoriously difficult to generate tangible normative ideas, to the extent that they can inform policy debate, from his work. Indeed, one of the most counterintuitive aspects of his theory is that his ethics are primarily descriptive rather than prescriptive: they do not tell us what to do, nor why one course of action is necessarily preferable to another (the peculiar challenge that this descriptive quality poses to questions of legal norms will be taken up in Chapter 3). Levinas made clear that he regarded it more important to know of the nature of the encounter with the other, rather than its substance.[34] Instead ethics describes an unconditional disposition towards alterity within the structure of the human subject. This disposition originates prior to legal (or moral or political) choices, prior to our conception of personal freedom and autonomy. Such an idea of ethics is therefore hardly intuitive. It could even be argued that the very term 'ethics' has received undue prominence in characterisations of Levinas's oeuvre. His most developed ethical theory, drawn most fully in his two major works, is never presented as a structure of ethics for the sake of ethics alone.

Conventional debates within jurisprudence are largely strangers to Levinas's work, but as noted near the beginning of the chapter he has received attention within what could broadly be called critical or interdisciplinary strands of legal theory. At least in its early North American incarnation, critical legal studies (CLS) was primarily concerned with exposing the politics and biases of legal processes, which had previously been masked by the ideology of legal neutrality. The formal logic of law was argued to be a mask for rules and judgments that were often arbitrary, contingent or politically instrumental. As such, particular modes of injustice could be revealed: political bias, sexual discrimination and racism were argued to be not so much promoted by individual legal actors, but actually woven into the institutional fabric of law itself. The targets of this sort of critique were typically specific practices and disciplines of the law. With a barely disguised glee, many traditional textbook writers on jurisprudence have since declared 'CLS' to be dead.[35] In a very limited sense, thinking specifically of the original North American CLS, they are probably correct. But what such eager diagnoses tend to ignore is the much more amorphous and prevailing influence of critical methodologies in the legal academy, including outside the United States, since then. In the early 1990s, an apparently 'postmodern' or poststructuralist strand of legal theory had emerged, concerned not so much with particular legal processes, but rather with the status of the law as a text, the uses of grammatology and deconstruction, and also with an ethical imperative.[36]

The turn to such modes of thinking allows for a concern about substantive injustices to be developed into a much more general attack on the structural inadequacies of law. It is not simply the case that the law might act as a shroud for the internal prejudices and biases of those who have monopolised its operations over previous centuries of legal doctrine. Rather than restricting focus merely to the substantive values being projected outwards, critique may turn to think about law's incapacity to hear the marginal claims coming inwards. The question here is not merely the hidden politics of the law, but also its constitutive inability to comprehend the significance of the other. Levinas has been deployed to help legal scholars understand a striking range of legal issues in this respect, including the plight of migrants, the nature of judicial activism, the origins of liability in private law, and the basis for a radicalised understanding of human rights. This book asks what might unite these disparate applications of Levinasian ethics to law, and considers the challenges that such an ethics faces within today's legal landscape. Those questions, along with a general discussion of how Levinas's philosophy can be transposed into ideas about legal reasoning, make up the central two chapters of this book. The latter two chapters take up a particular problematic, asking of the limits of Levinas's application to law when law is understood as part of a biopolitical model of liberal governance. Insofar as literature on biopolitics suggests a complicity between law and ontology, between legal norms and our totalising understanding of being, the closing chapters suggest that we may need to formulate an alternative means through which Levinas can help us understand the ethical relation against a backdrop of the pervasive efforts to regulate life. But before then, Chapter 2 offers an introductory analysis of Levinas's philosophical ideas.

Notes

1. Kelsen, *Pure Theory of Law*, p. 168.
2. Cornell, *The Philosophy of the Limit*, p. 107.
3. Ben-Dor, *Thinking About Law*, p. 30.
4. Alford, 'Levinas and Political Theory', p. 146.

5. Critchley, 'Five Problems in Levinas's View of Politics', p. 172.
6. For a leading study on the political context of Levinas's philosophy, see Caygill, *Levinas and the Political*.
7. Devlin, *The Enforcement of Morals*; Hart, *Law, Liberty and Morality*.
8. Hart, *The Concept of Law*, pp. 193–200.
9. Hart, 'Are There Any Natural Rights?', p. 175.
10. Hart, *Law, Liberty and Morality*.
11. Fitzpatrick, 'The Abstracts and Brief Chronicles of the Time', pp. 24–5.
12. Consider, for instance, Fisk, 'History and Reason in Rawls' Moral Theory'.
13. Rawls, *Political Liberalism*, pp. 49–50.
14. Dworkin, *Law's Empire*, p. 214.
15. Mouffe, *On the Political*, p. 11.
16. See Schmitt, *The Concept of the Political*.
17. Mouffe, *On the Political*, p. 12.
18. E.g. see Foucault's analysis of biopolitics in *Society Must Be Defended*.
19. See Peperzak, *Beyond*, pp. 198–200.
20. Derrida, *Of Grammatology*, p. 43.
21. Douzinas and Warrington with McVeigh, *Postmodern Jurisprudence*, p. 91.
22. Dworkin, *Law's Empire*; Dworkin, *Justice in Robes*; Dworkin, 'A Reply by Ronald Dworkin'.
23. Dworkin, *Taking Rights Seriously*, pp. 105–30.
24. Dworkin, *Law's Empire*, p. 272.
25. Such a depth of influence was evinced in Derrida's remark on Levinas, that 'I am ready to subscribe to everything he says' (Derrida and Labarriere, *Altérités*, p. 74).
26. Derrida, 'Force of Law'; Derrida, *The Gift of Death and Literature in Secret*; see also de Villes, *Law as Absolute Hospitality*, chapter 4.
27. Derrida, 'Force of Law', p. 963.
28. Derrida, *The Gift of Death*, p. 68.
29. See, e.g., Derrida, *Limited Inc*.
30. Dworkin, *Law's Empire*, pp. 273–5.
31. Derrida, *Adieu*, p. 23. Similarly, in *The Politics of Friendship*, he refers to the decision of the other, the 'absolute other in me, the other as the absolute that decides on me in me' (Derrida, *The Politics of Friendship*, p. 68).
32. Levinas, *Otherwise than Being*, p. 142.
33. This form of 'law' in Lacan came to be known by the shorthand

'Name-of-the-Father'. See Lacan, *The Seminar of Jacques Lacan: The Psychoses*.

34. Levinas, *Totality and Infinity*, p. 18.
35. E.g. McLeod, *Legal Theory*, pp. 155–6; Tamanaha, 'Conceptual Analysis, Continental Social Theory, and CLS'.
36. E.g. Douzinas and Warrington with McVeigh, *Postmodern Jurisprudence*; Douzinas and Warrington, *Justice Miscarried*; Cornell, *The Philosophy of the Limit*; Cornell et al., *Deconstruction and the Possibility of Justice*; Peter Fitzpatrick, *Dangerous Supplements*.

2

The Ethics of Emmanuel Levinas

Levinas's philosophy could be described as a theory of subjectivity first, and a theory of ethics second. If this observation stands up, it does so not only with respect to conceptual focus, but also chronology: his early works barely mention ethics at all. His ideas sprang out of a vehement critique of philosophies of ontology, where 'ontology' came to be defined by Levinas somewhat idiosyncratically as the reduction of the other to the same via a conception of being.[1] His thinking is preoccupied with the question of how we understand ourselves in our place in the world, but also the threshold of that understanding with respect to its beyond. The relation between being and otherwise-than-being marks the same structural opposition that he elsewhere describes as same/other, totality/infinity, interior/exterior. In each, the bounded and graspable nature of the first term is constituted within an ineluctable relation with the alterity of the second. The ethical nature of the human encounter derives from the manner in which it expresses this transcendent otherness. Before moving onto a more comprehensive journey through Levinas's philosophy, it should be useful to provide a workable outline of the core theory he had developed by the later stages of his life. What follows is highly condensed, but hopefully serves as a roadmap of where Levinas's ideas eventually arrived and the work done by some of his key themes.

By the time Levinas published his second major philosophical monograph in 1974, *Otherwise than Being or Beyond Essence*, he had produced a highly rigorous theory of subjectivity constituted out of language and time. Our relation with being is always a temporal relation. Levinas was interested in the way that being manifests itself to us, revealing a gap, a lapse in time that he calls being getting out of phase with itself. Time is recuperated or synchronised so as to express being's full, expansive essence. But Levinas asks whether, originating before this essence, we might trace the signification of diachronous time, a time of the other. The temporality that structures the exposition of being leaves a fragile imprint of being's other, which slips away from essence before it comes to presence. The temporality of ontology cannot be separated from language. Words are capable of expressing the presence of being, making claims that 'this is', or 'things are', and so on (the verb 'to be' expresses being's essence most succinctly). To the extent that language articulates a settled and shared distribution of meaning, or an economy of the same, Levinas describes it as 'the said'. Against this, Levinas poses the 'saying', a radical form of signification that originates in the other.

Levinas's analysis of language and time allows him to depict subjectivity as operating in exposure to alterity. This should not be understood merely physically, as one person's body being touched by another. The encounter with the other is not something that happens *to* the subject. Rather, Levinas regards subjectivity as being constituted by that very exposedness, and by the response that the other elicits. Saying is a form of exposure to the other. This saying is not an assertion of truth, transmitted from one entity to the other. Such discourse would express essence. Instead, saying is a form of discourse characterised by absolute passivity rather than intentionality (the significance of thought directed towards an entity). This leads Levinas to describe the relationship with the other with the term 'proximity' – as opposed to communion, or sameness, or some form of representable structural connection. It is via proximity that Levinas describes many of the specific, and often quite striking, dynamics of the relation with the other. The proximal other obsesses and even persecutes the subject, demanding response but indebting the subject further the more it answers, rather than allowing it to discharge its duty.

A crucial question that Levinas has to deal with here is how one can still regard oneself as a subject whilst being constituted in this radical, pre-ontological relation with alterity. Levinas does not regard this as a dissolution of subjectivity; the subject still takes form, has consciousness, through a form of 'drawing-in', or shoring up, which he calls hypostasis. But by arising out of the antecedent proximity, out of the pre-ontological signification of saying, the subject is hypostasised in an accusative form, lacking the autonomy and sovereignty proper to modern ideas of subjectivity, and instead produced as a form of constitutive accountability for the other. Substitution describes this sense of being an individual subject yet somehow being provoked by alterity prior to a sense of one's own consciousness. It is a process of expiation for the other whilst living in one's own skin. In this peculiar situation of having one's self yet being for the other, one is, in Levinas's view, effectively substituted for the other.

One has an identity that defines oneself, yet it is through the antecedent relation with the other that this identity is assigned. We can therefore appreciate why Levinas delineates subjectivity as torsion, trauma or eating away at oneself. One is hostage to the other.

All of which leaves the burning question of what an 'ethics' has to do with all of this. Whilst Levinas was happy to give his work a modest peppering with value-weighted terms such as 'goodness', it is important to understand that his ethics is principally descriptive. He provides an account of subjectivity that apprehends its own finitude, its being bound to its existence, and its peculiar relation with the infinitude of the beyond, provoking what he calls a responsibility for the other. The other signifies in a way that cannot present itself within being. The subject is exposed to the other, but cannot grasp or understand the other. The work of subjectivity – taking a position, sounding one's voice – is to assert oneself without the other, and allows for the sense of responsibility that attends such ontological violence. To assume oneself is to be complicit in the other's erasure. Yet this is not a total exclusion. Subjectivity is built upon this pre-ontological affective encounter with the other, meaning that the other is always inscribed in the very same that effaces it. Responsibility therefore emerges out of the inversion of identity and freedom: it is the ethical relation with the other that makes me *me*.

The Escaping of Being

By now it should be apparent that anyone seeking a fluffy, friendly model of pluralist or cosmopolitan ethics might be disappointed. Whilst the sobriety of his style had a habit of ebbing and flowing over the years, Levinas's idea of subjectivity is at times profoundly bleak, meditating on our deep existential solitude, analysing phenomenologies of weariness, fatigue, malaise and nausea, and characterising the relation with the other as obsessive and persecutory.[2] The reader is not offered a sermon on the social virtues of being nice. The ethical component of Levinas's theory, in which the subject displays an impossible yet indeclinable inclination to transcend itself in the infinitude of the other, arises instead out of the inadequacy of ontologies of the self.

Continental philosophy since the late nineteenth century might understandably be thought of as announcing the death of the subject. Certainly, the fully self-sufficient and self-possessive Cartesian 'I' cannot be supported by anyone who takes Nietzsche or Heidegger seriously, or, for that matter, Marx or Freud, Foucault or Derrida. Levinas shared much of this cynicism, once remarking that the egotic self and its capacity for 'dominating and integrating the totality of being' appears truly absurd in the genocidal history, especially the recent history, of our civilisations.[3] But Levinas was also attuned to the danger of nihilism. He counterposed the alternative risk of a turn to an anti-humanism that relinquishes hope in the human subject and confines our understanding of humanity to objective and anonymous materiality.[4] The ultimate hazard in such a trajectory is that humanity again becomes objectified and instrumentalised, this time not through an abuse of its own self-regard, but through a complete reversal that sees humanity reduced to the most clinical, dispassionate understanding of material forces. Levinas's position is to pose an inverted humanism that seeks to renew our faith in subjectivity, but only by structuring it in relation with the other. What makes us human, therefore, are not the faculties secured within the sovereign self, but the very ethical sensibility of the subject, which restlessly seeks the other.[5]

To flesh out Levinas's position, we need to dwell for a moment on Husserl and Heidegger. Not only are the two characters crucial to understanding Levinas's scholarly biography, but both give a sense of what Levinas's own thought would come to react against. He would frequently recall that whilst Husserl, then nearing retirement, had drawn him to study in Freiberg, it was the presence of Heidegger, who had recently published *Being and Time*, that left the more potent and lasting impact.[6] Nevertheless, Husserl's philosophy was the subject of Levinas's doctoral thesis, subsequently published as *The Theory of Intuition in Husserl's Phenomenology*, and Levinas would later bring Husserl's thought to a French readership as his translator.

Husserl's method – transcendental phenomenology, no less – had promised to go 'back to the "things themselves"'.[7] Things are not made meaningful to us because they emit some sort of essence of what they are, which we then sense passively. Instead, the meaning that we experience when apprehending the object is constituted by our own cognitive faculties. Meaning is therefore not derived solely from the object, but from the relation that exists between the object and the subject. For example, if we were to pick up a pebble on a cold winter's day, we could construct a meaningful sentence describing that event, such as 'the stone felt cold'. But this sentence is still meaningful, whether or not the stone really was cold, or whether we ever picked up the stone in the first place. This demonstrates both the interior intuition and intentionality of the subject. It is the intentional projection of intuition that confers meaning to the words without having lived the referential event itself. Understanding the relationship between the subject and the world of objects in this manner allowed Husserl to develop the idea of the 'transcendental ego': the *ego* is transcendent in that it is presupposed by the world of objects, whose meaning it provides. The world therefore exists for the subject. As Husserl explains in *Cartesian Meditations*, '[b]y my living, by my experiencing, thinking, valuing, and acting, I can enter no world other than the one that gets its sense and acceptance or status in and from me, myself'.[8]

Whilst Husserl considers how the interiority of the subject relates to the exteriority of the world beyond, it is clearly this interiority that generates the meaning of the outside. Despite Husserl's promise to go beyond language, to the things themselves, Levinas claims that his work relies problematically on an economy of 'linguistic signs in the constitution of meaning',[9] delineating the subject within an economy of sameness. Such a view of the subject experiencing the world as if the world exists for the subject fails to account for what Levinas felt was the real provocateur of human subjectivity, the experience of the radical other, that which is truly beyond constituted language. Therefore, argues Levinas, Husserl has not sufficiently returned to phenomenality itself; and furthermore, the importance of the constitutive impact of the other upon the subject is elided in his work.

It would be simplistic to say that Levinas turned from Husserl to Heidegger in absolute terms. But one can detect in Levinas's early work a general thematic movement in that direction, via growing dissatisfaction with Husserl.[10] Why? In short, Husserl questionably prioritised the realm of perception and intentionality and not, as Heidegger did, the way in which meaning is revealed through our relationship with our being. Further, Heidegger recognised, in a way that Husserl did not, the historicity of humanity, that philosophy should be mindful of our emplacement within a contingent situatedness.[11] Although Husserl seeks to return to the things themselves in his phenomenological method, he ends up privileging the intuitive, representative capability of the ego to solve the problem of knowledge of the external world.

Heidegger sought to address the question of how we understand our own being in his 1927 magnum opus *Being and Time*. The nature of this question elicits a distinction between, on the one hand, entities such as people and, on the other hand, their being.[12] One can think about the existence of entities at a superficial level in which they manifest as phenomena, which Heidegger calls the 'ontic'. But underlying this is an 'ontological' level of inquiry where one questions not just entities but the being of entities (ontology being characterised by Heidegger in rather different terms to its use by Levinas). The manner in which concrete lived

existence can be questioned with reference to its underlying ontological conditions is described by marrying these two levels in the 'ontico-
ontological'.[13] These rather abstract distinctions make more sense when
grounded in what Heidegger terms *Dasein*, the specifically human mode of
seeking to understand one's own being.[14] For *Dasein*, understanding being
ultimately addresses the very finitude of one's temporal existence, the fact
that we live within limited time that has a beginning and an end. Time is
expressed in the relation between a being and its being, such that 'when-
ever Dasein tacitly understands and interprets something like being, it
does so with *time* as its standpoint'.[15] Here, time cannot be thought of
simply as the familiar 'clock time' of seconds, minutes and hours; it must
be a question of time as such.

If Levinas's eventual critique of Husserl was that he privileged the
same whilst failing to recognise the importance of the other's impact upon
the self, then one can see why Heidegger would prove seductive to the early
Levinas. Heidegger addresses the problem of the relation of subject and
world not by subordinating one to the other, but by posing the two terms
as mutually constitutive. In fact, Heidegger sought to undermine the very
duality of subject and object, instead deploying the idea of *Dasein* as an
expression of 'being-in-the-world'.[16] It would not be long before Levinas
would make known his deep dissatisfaction with Heidegger's work, yet
his first publication on Heidegger evinces the depth of the latter's influence. Levinas's later attack on Heideggerian thinking must be understood
against the backdrop of fascism in Germany, as well as Heidegger's own
joining of the Nazi Party in 1933. Levinas would become critical of the
manner in which Heidegger would subordinate the question of humanity
to the question of being, a manoeuvre that risks the instrumentalisation of
human life in a way whose horror is revealed in the wake of Nazism. Yet
in 1932 Levinas published an enthusiastic essay titled 'Martin Heidegger
and Ontology'. Here, Levinas perceived Heidegger to be a supporter of
productively humanist ideas. The article, largely exegetical, links the concepts of 'being' and 'existence' with terms such as 'man' and 'humanity',
so as to claim that the '[u]nderstanding of being characterizes man not as
an essential attribute, but is man's very mode of being'.[17] This is clearly
at odds with how Levinas would come to characterise being later on. But
these early thoughts of his should not be dismissed. It would not be an
overstatement to say that Levinas's philosophical corpus continued as
a critical engagement (often unspoken) with the themes of being, time
and world, which cannot be expressed without the echoes of Heidegger
resounding in the background.

That Levinas reformulated his position is clear, and his minor effort at revisionism is tellingly exposed by the omission of a sympathetic reference to Heideggers's 'theory of personality and freedom' in a 1949 abridgement of his 1932 essay.[18] By that time, Levinas had no faith in ontology as a path to freedom. This idea that freedom must be thought otherwise than via being began to percolate through his writings as early as 1935, when *De l'evasion* (translated into English as *On Escape*) made it into print. This would be the first serious articulation of Levinas's critique of ontology, which becomes characterised as a lonely and empty binding to the very facticity of being. Its very first sentence laments 'the brutal fact of being that assaults ... [human] freedom'.[19] He attacks what he perceives as the bourgeois subject whose self-satisfaction in its being nourishes and is nourished by conservatism and capitalism. Levinas describes the relationship with being as one of constraint within oneself. One is riveted to the fact of being, whose bare neutrality places it beyond any question of perfection or imperfection, good or bad, ideal or material: it simply is. Being supports this bourgeois subject by securing it against its own duality, and insuring it against a radical future that would disrupt the plenitude of the present.[20]

Against this Levinas poses the need to escape, to get out of this enchainment to the banality of existence, and to get out of oneself. This is articulated through an analysis of various drives and experiences centred around the human body. In pursuing our needs we may encounter the experience of pleasure. Achieving pleasure offers the possibility of escape; it breaks up the continuity of time; it allows us to momentarily forget ourselves. Yet it is never permanent, and we are always returned back to the instant in which we left, reduced to the experience of shame in being riveted still to ourselves, and ultimately delivered to the feeling of nausea. This nausea is experienced in the fullness of being from which we have not escaped, where '[w]e are revolted from the inside; our depths smother beneath ourselves; our innards "heave"'.[21]

Upon this view, subjectivity is determined purely by what is possessed and what simply *is*, and merely 'expresses the sufficiency of the fact of being, whose absolute and definitive character no one, it seems, could place in doubt'.[22] Levinas characterises this experience as one of imprisonment: one is imprisoned *by* being. Being is regarded as a burden upon oneself, an impediment to freedom.[23] Levinas is dissatisfied by the totalising effect of ontology in Heidegger's work. Even when structured by time, the finitude of being still restricts, constrains and burdens the subject. Levinas's innovation here is to see being as part of the problem, not part of the solution. We do not reach a freer and more authentic mode of existence by uncovering the essence of what it means to be. The problem is not a lack of being but, on the contrary, being's plenitude.[24] It is with these arguments that Levinas begins to develop the idea of an inclination to transcend oneself as an element of the human condition. He therefore poses the need for escape from being as a basic horizon of subjectivity, in which we seek 'to break that most radical and unalterably binding of chains, the fact that the I is oneself'.[25]

The themes of escape and of the stark horror of being were revisited in *Existence and Existents*,[26] initially published shortly after the war and based largely on various notes that Levinas wrote whilst in captivity. Levinas also built upon these ideas in a series of lectures in 1946–7, delivered at the newly established *Collège Philosophique* in Paris (eventually published as *Time and the Other*). The narrative of each of these pieces draws the reader through Levinas's emergent critique of ontology to arrive at a fresher thesis on subjectivity, temporality, and the other. He opens *Existence and Existents* with a familiar distinction between being and beings – or between, respectively, 'existence' and 'existents'. His thought on their relation is presented immediately in stark and unequivocal terms:

> Being is essentially alien and strikes against us. We undergo its suffering embrace like the night, but it does not respond to us. There is pain in Being.[27]

Revealing both his critical distance from Heidegger and the latter's influence, Levinas seeks to evoke the way that a being apprehends the facticity of being within which it finds itself. The existent that apprehends their existence is made weary by this very experience. Existence provokes the opposite of inspiration, motivation and vitality, and hangs around the neck of every being as if it were an obligation, such that it 'is like the remainder of a commitment to exist, with all the seriousness and harshness of an unrevocable contract'.[28] Existence is therefore presented as an imposition upon beings. Resonant with his thinking from the mid-1930s, it may make us want to escape, or may make us want to idly shut out its demand and stay in bed instead.[29] But existence, inescapable as it is, makes us work; it commits us to effort and labour. What is more, we do not find ourselves dissolved within the efforts of existence. Rather, we lag behind in what Levinas terms fatigue: a temporal gap between existence and a being whose effort never quite catches it up. Effort, therefore, condemns one to 'the present that lags behind the present'.[30]

This idea of a lapse in the temporality of being is obviously comparable with the structure of *Dasein*. Both Levinas and Heidegger are concerned with a foundational relationship between the being and being (or between the existent and existence), and both find time to be crucial to its understanding. Again, we can see that what for Heidegger signals the exposition of being as a path to authenticity, Levinas interprets through pejorative phenomenological terms as a limitation on the human subject. But is there anything more than a fundamental disagreement about the potential of ontology here? Heidegger prioritises the ontological over the ontic, the underlying realm of being over the world of immediate appearances and representations. For example, the ontological significance of a tool for *Dasein* is not simply its disposable status as a thing, but the chain of referrals from which the tool is derived. The tool refers back to metal and wood, and to mountains and forests, and so on.[31] Writing at a time when he was more sympathetic to Heidegger, Levinas explained the virtues of this approach: '[t]he totality of referrals which constitutes the tool's *being* leads us thus well above the very narrow sphere of usual objects that surrounds us'.[32] Yet the later, anti-Heideggerian Levinas asks why one would or should trace objects such as tools back to their being, representing 'an ontological finality, to which he [Heidegger] subordinates objects in the world'.[33] By this, Levinas introduces the idea that relations with objects need not be inauthentic or insincere. When we eat, or read, or play a game with a ball, this action can be sincere without the need for concern for being. Levinas laments the idea that we do not do these things simply for their own sake, the sum of which makes up life itself.[34] A life orientated around a care for being itself sounds to Levinas like a life of banal perseverance, as devoid of meaning as it would be devoid of enjoyment.[35]

The prioritisation of being takes one away from the travails of everyday life, which Heidegger may call inauthentic but which Levinas would identify as part of the very vitality of life itself, and into an altogether more sinister realm. When being reigns over the being(s), there is a state of what Levinas terms 'existence without existents'. Alternatively, it is the *there is* [*il y a*], or more explicitly, 'being in general'.[36] Numerous evocative phrases elucidate the way in which the *there is* appears in Levinas's thought, none of them flattering. It is impersonal and anonymous,[37] it is a 'rustling' horror,[38] it invades and overwhelms experience,[39] and is like the reign of the night that conquers the insomniac.[40] When afflicted by insomnia one is riveted by being itself.[41] Heidegger is not entirely a stranger to apprehensiveness towards being; his analytic of anxiety describes the evocation of care in the face of nothingness, or of death.[42] But this is fear *for* being. What Levinas describes is fear *of* being itself, from which we cannot escape.[43]

Hypostasis

Insomnia represents the development of Levinas's earlier metaphor of nausea. As Jacques Rolland observes, nausea, like insomnia, is the experience of the submerging of the existent in existence, where the latter appears as a pervasive and oppressive presence.[44] In order to understand how Levinas poses the escape from this, and thus structures subjectivity in its disposition towards the transcendent other, it is necessary to revisit Levinas's concept of time. The time of the *there is* is posed as pure duration without end. But its beginningless and endless temporality is ruptured by the event that Levinas calls hypostasis. If insomnia represents the dissolution of subjectivity in anonymous, expansive being, hypostasis effects the opposite, drawing the subject in on itself. Subjectivity needs a home. Occupying a place is the first condition of hypostasis posed in *Existence and Existents*, and the most elementary place is the corporeal body.[45] But more importantly, hypostasis involves having a hold on time.[46] The present is the event by which the subject claims a time of its own, whereby it grasps and masters the situation around it. In *Time and the Other*, the present 'is a rip in the infinite beginningless and endless fabric of existing'.[47] The hypostasis therefore marks the end of existence without existents, and the moment of mastery of existence *by* the existent – still burdened with the weight of existence, but no longer lost in its anonymity.[48]

Emerging in a position and time of its own, the subject experiences freedom. However, this is a lonely freedom. Out of the anonymous *there is* the subject claims its identity, but it is alone and 'chained to its self'[49] (the metaphor of enchainment to oneself begins in *On Escape*[50] and survives right up to Levinas's later work, in particular *Otherwise than Being*[51]). The question of how this solitude and enchainment is broken is addressed through the opening of time as the encounter with alterity. The *there is* presents a vacuous and interminable time, against which the subject in hypostasis claims a graspable present. But a much more meaningful experience of time is felt in the beyond of that present, as 'the absolute alterity of another instant'.[52] The hypostatic gesture is, of course, a condition of this experience of the diachronous time of the other. It is only by having a hold on the present that one can apprehend the absolute otherness of other times. It is for this reason that Levinas's extended meditation on the drawing-in of the subject is essential.

The other opens the fullest experience of time, as a horizon towards which the subject seeks to escape its enchainment to itself. The nature of the other's embodiment is afforded considerable explication in *Time and the Other*, in the manner that death and alterity are considered together. Unlike Heidegger, who saw death as a conditioning element of authenticity, Levinas found a different significance for death in its absolutely unknowable nature, its excess of the limits of the subject. The terms of this limit means that, contra Heidegger, the apprehension of death does not effect activity over the self, but passivity of the self.[53] Death therefore 'indicates that we are in relation with something that is absolutely other',[54] and furthermore, death has a distinctly futural character. Time is not a linear procession of instants by which we break down days into hours, minutes and seconds, and nor is it the presence of a flow by which instants lose their independence. Rather, it is the relation with other times, with the alterity of futures and pasts, as they are embodied in the social. Time is sociality.

The difference between this view of the relation with otherness and Heidegger's view was drawn more clearly in the 1951 article, 'Is Ontology Fundamental?'[55] Of course, for Heidegger ontology *is* fundamental, and so the other being becomes meaningful only with reference to being. One's understanding of others, in this context, must therefore be predicated upon some level of pre-understanding (as the individual being is understood through being in general). This involves letting the being be, allowing themselves to reveal themselves in being. This may be all well and good for a lifeless object, but Levinas argues that this is simply an erroneous way of conceiving a human-human relation. One does not understand the other ontologically in advance of addressing them except by assimilating their very otherness. The approach to/of the other precedes and evades any form of understanding or misunderstanding of the other's being (and of being as such). It therefore also precedes ontology itself. The other person is the embodiment of radical alterity which opens the possibility of time by effacing the totality of being. Time does not disclose the other as part of a common terrain of being – at least, not without reducing the other to the same. The addressing of the other is, for Levinas, an affective experience more immediate than ontological (mis)understanding and, in any case, is by no means exhausted by any notion of understanding as such. Therefore, Levinas characterises one's relationship with the other as religious rather than being ontological.[56] One must be cautious to qualify how Levinas uses this idea of religion. It should not be understood as Levinas's transmutation from philosopher to theologian with respect to these ideas. Nor should it require Levinas's withdrawal from questions of secular politics. As he explains quite modestly, this term is simply meant to indicate that the relation with the other can be explicated and can be meaningful without being reduced to a relation of knowledge, and without its essence being given in advance.[57] And it is this relation that is at the heart of the human subject.

Although these early texts of Levinas's lack the mature rigour of his later writings, one can clearly see a consistent set of thematic patterns. In each, Levinas sketches subjectivity's contraction and break-up, an idea of its release from being, a release that never truly escapes being, and is not orientated toward any other determinate place – only toward escape itself. Against the reductivism of Husserl and Heidegger, whose work Levinas sees as demanding a return to the same, Levinas's prioritisation of a non-assimilative and non-reductive relation with the other would show his thought to be typically 'Judaic'. By contrast, upon Derrida's interpretation, both Husserl and Heidegger, in the 'shadow' of Hegel, are 'dominated' by 'Greek' thought.[58] Such Greek thought represents a tradition of reducing philosophy to a dichotomy of subject-object, or inside-outside, which in turn privileges the concept of light: that which makes the object accessible to the subject.[59] This reduction takes different forms (for example, phenomenological, ontological), but all variants demonstrate this common root. On the contrary, Levinas seeks to liberate metaphysics, claiming that a meaningful idea of transcendence can only be found outside the Greek tradition.[60] For Heidegger everything is placed under the question of illumination in our experience of being in the world – the unthought may come to be thought, the misunderstood understood, the concealed revealed. Derrida describes this as 'the violence of light',[61] the idea that everything is illuminable. By contrast, for Levinas the relation with the other is not an exposition, but an address; the other is radically and inexorably separate, not known in relation to being, but only proximal.

'Are we Jews? Are we Greeks?': Levinas's two masterworks

The point of departure which opens the argument of *Totality and Infinity* is explained in the initial few pages, where Levinas explains how '[t]he visage of being that shows itself in war is fixed in the concept of totality, which dominates Western philosophy'.[62] War is the unavoidable consequence of the reign of ontology, for ontology cannot resist totalisation, the urge or ambition to say *what is*, whose politicisation is the 'mobilization of absolutes'.[63] A claim over being itself would be impotent if it did not deign to destroy all counter-claims, and this opens the field of war that enlists people against their will. Against war, Levinas contrasts eschatology, described as 'a relationship with a *surplus always exterior to the totality*'.[64] Infinity is the concept by which Levinas refers to that which exceeds and transcends the totality that ontology must depend upon. One must note, however, that infinity is not a state into which one may ascend or dissolve, out of totality, in a kind of metaphysical nirvana. Instead, infinity is produced within totality.[65]

Levinas's ultimate project in *Totality and Infinity* is to mount a 'defence of subjectivity',[66] posing the latter not as an egotic self that understands the world through totality and as for itself, nor as a pawn in the machinations of ontological war, or dissolved into the sea as anti-humanism predicted, but through an eschatological drive that locates the idea of infinity in the subject itself. This is to propose a metaphysics that is predicated on desire: the idea of infinity in the subject corresponds to a desire of the other. If we are not to be trapped in totality, the idea of infinity is necessary. Furthermore, infinity requires us to understand the nature of the difference between same and other.[67] If the other is the embodiment of infinity, and if infinity denotes the very excess of being that ontology denies, then it must be radically separate. Therefore, what allows the subject to apprehend itself in its own finitude is the very infinitude of the other.

More work is required before Levinas can justify his claim that subjectivity holds within itself an eschatological drive and, with it, a desire of the other. He embarks on a long discussion of how, first, the subject is individuated in its frail autonomy. In line with the arguments made in *On Escape*, *Existence and Existents*, and *Time and the Other*, possession and, before it, habitation draw the being out of its subordination to being and grant it enjoyment in its drawing in upon itself. Yet it is precisely this possession that is then put into question by the shattering encounter with the other. That we exist as separated beings (and this is necessary in Levinas's critique of totality) means that the encounter with the other person has a radical impact on one's sense of propriety. The 'ethical' relation with the other, which is central to subjectivity, is dutiful, demanding apology, judgment and responsibility. Central to *Totality and Infinity* is Levinas's use of the face as an expression of the encounter with the other. The face is that which, without *presenting* the other or making it graspable or an object of knowledge, expresses its exteriority, its absolute otherness, implied by infinity. The face calls into question the possession, sovereignty and freedom of the self. Under accusation, the subject undergoes an ethical injunction to restrain its own ontological violence, what Levinas repeatedly invoked through the commandment not to kill. Whilst one may dwell upon many of the unequivocally valuable results of the ethical relation (goodness, truth, justice, reason, for example) it may be especially deserving to emphasise how it defines a more meaningful freedom. In line with the argument of *Time and the Other*, freedom here is found in the time of the other. Therefore, while many of the themes in this work, and in many of Levinas's works, seem at first to allude to subjugation (apology, responsibility, guilt, and so on) they are also the condition of the very freedom of the human subject.

In the thirteen years that bridged *Totality and Infinity* and *Otherwise than Being*, Levinas had come to appreciate some concerns that he would seek to address in the latter work. The preface to the 1987 German edition of the former provides some clues as to the different ambitions of the two books. We are told that *Otherwise than Being* 'avoids the ontological – or more exactly, *eidetic* – language which *Totality and Infinity* incessantly resorts to'.[68] In other words, the earlier work had focused on the experience of phenomena (something for which Levinas reproached Husserl). Part of what inspired the change of emphasis in *Otherwise than Being*, especially the move away from the explicitly acknowledged phenomenological language, was the publication of Derrida's 'Violence and Metaphysics'.[69] The themes in Husserl and Heidegger that Levinas seeks to escape from are, ironically, repeated in *Totality and Infinity* itself. Derrida suggests sceptically that Levinas talks within the Greek language in his attempt to undermine it.[70] Levinas wants to describe the encounter with and the significance of the other, before the violent (pre)comprehension of the other that he identifies in Husserl and Heidegger. Yet he remains within a terminology that stifles this ambition. For example, he uses the concept of 'exteriority' to denote a non-site of the other, a space of the other that is not a space, and is thus not within the grasp of the same.[71] This prompts Derrida to challenge Levinas on the necessity of using a graspable spatial term to describe something that is purportedly non-spatial.[72]

Bettina Bergo has reviewed a number of commentaries on the shift in emphasis and method between the two works. Specifically she is interested in the manner in which the idea of the real social relation with the other in *Totality and Infinity* yields to a theory of a subjectivity constituted by the paradoxically immanent 'presence' of the transcendent other already within the subject in *Otherwise than Being*.[73] That is, an analysis of a classic subject-object relation (as between subject and other in this context) turns to that of a relation between the subject and the radical non-phenomenal other within itself. She takes support from Stephan Strasser who, she claims, argues that a relationship that is reciprocal (in dialogue or teaching, for instance) and eidetic (in the phenomenology of the face) becomes in *Otherwise than Being* an immanent relation, not with a phenomenon, but with 'an absence, a gap in the structure of the world'.[74] Similarly, Adriaan Peperzak observed that the concept of the self in particular is changed between the two works. In the former, the self is described in its enjoyment of the world, prior to the relation with the other, which is the locus of the ethical. In *Otherwise than Being* however, the self is the ethical locus.[75]

In any case, *Otherwise than Being* returns to an emphasis on being that evokes his much earlier works such as *On Escape* and *Existents and Existence*. Being is identified early on as 'essence', which, in the Heideggerian tradition, allows one to distinguish being from beings.[76] Further, we are told that 'essence is interest'.[77] Interest would refer to the capacity of being to endure and make sense of the world, to fill all voids, to reverberate and enunciate itself: it is 'the persisting in being'.[78] Being is characterised as an enduring schema of meaning, '[b]ut what is *Being's other?*' asks Levinas.[79] As in *Totality and Infinity*, Levinas presupposes a transcendence that exceeds ontology: to being Levinas opposes the otherwise than being. But the conceptual framework that was previously dominated by phenomenological method is replaced with an analytic of language (the 'saying' and the 'said') and – once again – a renewed interest in time (synchrony and diachrony).

Levinas tells us a lot in the dense and enigmatic claim that '[b]eing's essence is the temporalization of time, the diastasis of the identical and its recapture or reminiscence, the unity of apperception'.[80] First, again, Levinas sees being and time as intimately related. An understanding of being must address its temporality, its ability to persist through time, and moreover (and inversely) the precondition of temporality to its persistence (the latter, again, a distinctly Heideggerian theme). However, what is being alluded to with the terms 'diastasis', 'recapture', 'reminiscence' and 'apperception' is that this temporality involves the continual lapse and then synchronisation of time. Synchrony denotes the eerie dominance of being whose horror is described by Levinas in *Existence and Existents*. And recalling in particular the argument in *Time and the Other*, for there to be time there must be diachrony, i.e. the lapse, times getting 'out of phase' with one another, the alterity of one instant to another. Time requires both synchrony and diachrony. And the essence or interest of being is this synchronisation or recapture of time, the reduction of diachrony, that renders everything intelligible in the 'unity of apperception' or full consciousness.

Levinas articulates the relationship of being and time via language. As Paul Ricoeur once said, the book's central wager is to explicate a relation of 'Saying on the side of ethics, the said on the side of ontology'.[81] It is necessary to explain the groundwork underlying this distinction. Levinas talks of the verb to be, and the way that this refers to be-ing, the flow of time through being, or the very temporality of being.[82] Language expresses the play of synchrony and diachrony, specifically through the saying and the said. The said resembles what has already been said. It is signification that refers to what is already known. To signify an entity through the said is to signify it with a concept that preceded and constituted the entity's very identification. In this case the signification, or 'saying', synchronises; that is, it is correlative with the said, and serves to 'coagulate the flow of time into a "something"'.[83] But this is not the only type of saying. If subjectivity is something other than the enslaved articulation of a pre-existent ontology, and if time itself should be meaningful, there must be a dimension of saying that does not defer to a said, and which signifies diachrony. What is the nature of the saying prior to the said? This, Levinas explains, is the expression of the element of the human experience that provokes us into ethical responsibility for the otherwise-than-being.[84]

Levinas argues that saying has a primacy over the said. If the said is settled meaning, knowledge, synchrony, ontology and so on, and if the saying is a disruptive, diachronic excess, then it is forgivable that one might think to prioritise the former as a means of correcting the latter and entering it into knowledge. This is not the case for Levinas. It is the latter, saying, which is fundamental, and only 'starting with subjectivity in the form of saying, the signification of the said will be interpretable'.[85] In other words, we only have a said because we first have a saying. Otherwise than Being's central argument centres around the claim that '[s]aying states and thematizes the said ... with a signification that has to be distinguished from that borne by words in the said', and that this signification operates in a relation of proximity, which 'is quite distinct from every other relationship, and has to be conceived as a responsibility for the other; it might be called humanity, or subjectivity, or self'.[86] Whilst these ideas explicitly talk of a relation with the other, this is of a more complex form than that encountered in Totality and Infinity and, as we already know, is demanded by his attempt to think a relation with the other that escapes the traps of traditional phenomenology. What, then, is the nature of this 'relation' to the other in Otherwise than Being? Saying is more fundamental than the said, but it is irruptive and diachronic.[87] One may then ask what provokes this surprising character of the saying. The answer is the other, structured *in* subjectivity itself, as 'the other in the same',[88] as some sort of constitutive lack that calls the subject into radical signification without deference to the ontological said. Saying addresses itself to another being, but this other is not the 'object' that the subject apprehends, but is embedded within the subject itself. In this sense, Levinas takes a view of language alien to those who would, understandably, hold 'saying' to originate from a spontaneity of the egotic self.[89] This relation with the other, which is not really a relation in any conventional sense, is what Levinas means by proximity. As noted above, Levinas associates proximity with responsibility, which will eventually be illuminated as the obsessive process of substituting oneself for the other, inverting autonomy. Having now given an overview of the basic contentions about subjectivity and ethics in Levinas's two masterworks, the remainder of the chapter will attempt to speak across their respective and rather different forms and methods to address several common themes. These themes describe recurring preoccupations in Levinas's thinking, despite often manifesting through slightly varied terminologies. The following sections will consider Levinas's thoughts on restlessness, temporality and asymmetry, as well as the intellectual significance of his Judaism.

Restlessness

A subject that is absolutely autonomous is able to sit comfortably. It has no concern other than itself. The Levinasian subject, on the other hand, has a hold on itself, but is always troubled by the other. It is restless. The constitutive relation with the other never provides satisfaction. Being can never be truly escaped, infinity never truly reached, the other never grasped. Yet the subject is always in a state of internal provocation, undermined not by an approach from the outside, as if one could avoid it by hiding oneself away, but at its very foundation.

If a relation with infinity is only possible from a position of separation, then separation must be maintained through works of interiority, allowing the same-other relationship to make sense. This however, is opposed to a being that is subordinated to being, to 'the totalization of history'.[90] What is such a work of interiority, which manifests separation, which in turn is implicit in the very idea of infinity? Levinas argues that separation arises first in the enjoyment that grants a sense of self-sufficiency.[91] Enjoyment is derived from needs; and what we need is what we live from. That we need is by no means the same as an unhappy lack, and does not suggest a dependency contrary to happiness.[92] This should not appear too controversial if one considers the example of food. One needs food, yet this does not prevent eating from being an enjoyable activity. Nor does eating eradicate one's need for food: enjoyment is found in satisfaction of need, not its eradication.[93] The things we enjoy are not mere tools, and have significance beyond being referred back to being itself.[94]

The restlessness of the subject becomes apparent when Levinas describes the state of interiority as not absolutely closed. Separation and enjoyment are, after all, invoked as necessitated by the idea of infinity and the transcendence of the other. Yet metaphysical desire, the desire of the other, is distinct from need – the latter being satiable, reducing other to same and producing happiness, the former being insatiable and maintaining the radicality of the desired's transcendence.[95] The state of the separated being is defined by Levinas in *Totality and Infinity* as the dwelling, which allows the subject to close in on itself but without fully closing off the beyond that lies outside.[96] By being both open and closed, the dwelling therefore incorporates two apparently contrary characteristics which do not have any dialectical link. On the one hand it is the very site of one's autonomy. It allows for the possession of things; it allows things to be 'laboured' upon and have their independence inverted and turned into an existence for the subject. Once a thing becomes held, possessed and understood as an object that furnishes the dwelling, it becomes a term of ontology.[97] But what is more curious about the dwelling is the other characteristic, its openness. The dwelling welcomes, but what is welcomed inside first is the subject itself. The familiarity of the world which the dwelling offers does not begin from the subject but from an other. This initial welcome into the dwelling is before all this a welcome from a different form of other than encountered in the face-to-face, marked not by 'you'/'*vous*' but 'thou'/'*tu*', by intimacy rather than height, and, importantly, by a specifically feminine grace and gentleness.[98] The condition of dwelling is not spontaneous self-creation, nor is it a Heideggerian 'throwness' into the world. Instead, it is 'a recollection, a coming to oneself, a retreat home with oneself as in a land of refuge, which answers to a hospitality, an expectancy, a human welcome'.[99]

Via this oddly and unnecessarily gendered concept, Levinas claims the woman signifies that which welcomes the subject to 'oneself'. The feminine welcome into the home is the condition of all the self-mastery that the home would allow. To take a place (such as a dwelling) involves denying it to an-other.[100] The egology of the separated being demands it be able to represent to itself that which it lives from. A withdrawal is needed for this representation to take place, which is characterised via the encounter with the woman who welcomes. Dwelling is also the condition of the possession of property, and allows one to take a distance from one's possessions in order to represent and cognise them. But this distance, the way that we place ourselves 'above' our property, means we must also encounter the other that embodies transcendence and infinity, a figure that radically puts into question the propriety of one's relation with the dwelling.[101]

Restlessness here is found in the way the dwelling describes one's autonomy being both open and closed, providing a sense of place yet always challenged by the transcendent other.[102] The condition of having a grasp on oneself is the very calling into question of that grasp's propriety. This tension, in which autonomy is necessary but never absolute, is revisited with greater nuance in *Otherwise than Being*, through the concepts of passivity, proximity and substitution. Passivity is the idea through which Levinas initially explains the affective nature of subjectivity, the way in which it is exposed to alterity. The radical nature of this passivity is necessary if Levinas is to eventually convince the reader of the unconditional and seemingly limitless nature of responsibility to the other. Meanwhile, responsibility, the manner in which the subject finds itself under accusation from the other, is not assumed voluntarily and appears precisely by virtue of this passivity.[103] Therefore one's relation with the other, the exposure that signifies as saying and without deference to the ontological said, does not arise out of free or conscious choice. Rather, the basis of saying is this surprising signification where one passively finds oneself bound to the other. Consciousness is described by Levinas as 'the naïve spontaneity of the ego': it is not a state of wisdom and rationality, but a naïve state whose arrogance is undermined by a prior passivity that allows the other to put one's freedom into question.[104]

To find oneself responsible for the other, in a responsibility that precedes consciousness, to find one's very subjectivity owed to the other, is naturally traumatic. Saying is the exposure of the subject to the other; it is communication where the subject does not express a sign, but becomes one. Just as the dwelling is a refuge rather than a position of absolute sovereignty, the subject is constitutively uprooted, or constituted in its own torsion.[105] Levinas makes clear that the responsibility for the other is not a gentle, harmonious relation. Instead, subjectivity finds itself in its own undoing.

Passivity is quickly elaborated by Levinas through themes of sensibility and vulnerability, and then further into pain and suffering, all of which denote the way in which the subject is precisely a subjection. If the absolutely autonomous subject is marked by strength, in its capacity for self-ascription and self-identification, the ethical subject that Levinas describes is notable for its apparent weakness, its incapacity for self-sufficiency, and its inability to enjoy itself without finding itself (before any time of choice) torn from itself.[106] Insofar as we might use 'one' to denote the subject, one not only is susceptible to pain, but one *is* pain, one *is* being torn from oneself. This is the condition of the subject's constitutive passivity.

Sensibility is exposure to the other. Or put another way, it is the importance of the other for the subject, the 'other in the same' that constitutes subjectivity. Ethical signification occurs primarily on the basis of sensibility, and not on the basis of intentionality (contra Husserl)[107] or on the basis of being (contra Heidegger).[108] Understandably then, the condition of sensibility is proximity – one must be proximate to that which is sensed, after all. Proximity should not be thought of in geometric terms, however.[109] It does not describe a spatial formation of people living close to one another. Nor is it a state of being that upon conscious reflection demands one behaves generously; but rather, proximity is restlessness.[110] Proximity places the subject in an approach. This approach, however, never arrives at what it seeks: it is only a caress and never a grasp.[111] Proximity denotes the signification for the other, the diachronic rupture of synchrony in which the subject takes responsibility for the other, yet takes responsibility without the other being reduced to the same.[112] Thus the pure signification of exposure, the signification for the other, is formulated *as* proximity.[113] The disruption of the said by the saying, or the synchronic by the diachronic, is anarchic in nature and as such not governed by any representable concept which, by its essence, would be of the order of the said, or of the synchronic.[114]

Otherwise than Being's chapter on substitution tries to answer the question of how the subject can still be described as a subject when constituted by its own undoing. The question is, if the restless subject is the one whose foundation is undermined by its debt to the other (whose foundation *is* the debt to the other), how can we still call this a subject? The paradox or aporia identified in this question is embodied by what Levinas calls the 'oneself'. It is with this term that he describes and develops the idea of a subject that maintains or ascribes itself whilst, paradoxically, having been originally assigned by alterity. Again, the significance of the other for the subject is difficult and traumatic, suffering a persecution that intervenes to prevent the oneself from assuming autonomy.[115] The subjectivity of the oneself is to be born into one's own body, yet to discover that one must take responsibility for another in accordance with a debt prior to birth.

The gathering in of the oneself for itself, equivalent to the image of the dwelling in *Totality and Infinity*, carries a degree of artifice. It is a term not of authenticity, but of hypostasis. The terms of the said, or the essence of being, which allow a subject to represent itself do not provide access to an authentic mode of existence, but grant intelligibility at the price of veiling the otherwise-than-being. The tension between the need to have an ontological grasp on things and the fundamental provocation of the other that escapes this grasp is expressed in the idea that the oneself functions in 'recurrence'.[116] Recall Levinas's concept of shame in *On Escape*: the awkward return to self and the need for apology. In the same way, recurrence describes this painful inwardness of the subject, burdened with itself, yet indebted to the other. There is torsion in recurrence, an 'anguish' in which recurrence means being oneself whilst at the same time inverting oneself.[117]

If one's subjectivity is constituted by the other – or to put it another way, if one exists through the other – then one is substituted for the other, because it is through the other that one's subjectivity is lived. The subject is not limited by an autonomous identity, and is freed into responsibility. In this sense 'identity is inverted'.[118] Substitution denotes the manner in which the subject finds itself in the other, in the torsion and trauma of being structured as the other in the same. This torsion never relents, because despite the subject finding itself in the other, this falls far short of a true escape. One finds freedom in responsibility,[119] but it is not a freedom that represents one's absolute sovereignty or transcendence of the self.[120] We can therefore understand the seemingly paradoxical claim of Levinas that '[i]n substitution my being that belongs to me and not to another is undone, and it is through this substitution that I am not "another", but me'.[121] Therefore, whilst the subject is substituted, it is far from being dissolved into the infinitude of alterity. Substitution on the contrary affirms the very subjectivity of the subject, assigns the subject as responsible, and does nothing to erase the potency of ipseity, other than to determine it as traumatically indebted to the other. Substitution does not dissolve identity, but constitutes it.

Temporality

Much has already been said about time, such is its importance for Levinas's thinking, but a few further broad comments can be made on the subject of past, future and death. The temporality of life, Levinas explains in

Totality and Infinity, is having time, postponing death rather than being for death.[122] It is to apprehend death yet to be against it. The role of the other here is somewhat complex. To exist in a multiplicity is risky. It is to exist within totality, which appears a safe ontological distribution, and yet to be exposed to the risk of violence that the other poses. Death, whose postponement is the condition of time and freedom itself, is unknowable. We do not have a countdown to our expiration. Therefore, death and the other come from the same place.[123] The answer is not to withdraw from the relation with the other and face the death that the other threatens. Although 'courageous', this simply makes the being serve the other in death rather than life.[124] The other, coming from the same 'region' as death, offers the possibility of postponement of death, or even of a time beyond death.[125] It therefore offers time itself, and the freedom that can be found in the latter. The desire of the other that opens up, leads to the modalities of apology, judgment and responsibility.

Totality and Infinity introduces the idea of infinite time, an irruptive, discontinuous time opposed both to linear clock time and to the Heideggerian notion of a time constituted by being.[126] It is infinite time that holds the possibility of breaking out of the time of totality and history, and which meets the aspirations of eschatology, of a future undetermined by ontology. In the final pages before *Totality and Infinity*'s conclusion, Levinas evokes a double bind between infinite time and 'messianic' time.[127] This latter time, the messianic, is necessary for the political, as politics requires a greater certainty than the irruptive, futural and risky infinite time. Yet this messianism, this hope for the good and the guarding against evil, inevitably relies on infinite time to present it with its very possibilities.

The analytic of time made in *Otherwise than Being* represents a terminological shift and a conceptual refocusing. The responsive, responsible saying, addressed to the other, signifies diachronously. Nevertheless, the manner in which this ruptures synchrony, the said, and therefore history itself, reveals the resonance with *Totality and Infinity*. It is important to recall that time for Levinas is not represented as a linear flow, but as radical difference: the alterity of times to each other. The relation with the other describes a temporal lapse between the other and the same. Here, Levinas introduces the significance not merely of the future, but also of the past. The provocation of the other comes from a time already passed, yet not one that we could measure with a clock or calendar, but an originary time that precedes our very consciousness and freedom.[128] This notion of an accusation that resonates as an echo of a time that we have missed describes an important aspect of the responsibility that Levinas explicates in *Otherwise than Being*. What characterises our guilt, and what prompts us to enter the traumatic experience of substitution in pursuing our responsibility, is that we are late, that we have survived the other's absence.[129] The other leaves a trace from the 'immemorial past'[130] from which it originates; but it is not here, or rather, not now.

Asymmetry

The relation with the other is asymmetrical. This was presented in an almost literal, spatial sense in *Totality and Infinity*, where the infinitude of the other expresses a position of height over the subject. But asymmetry also denotes other forms of inequality, primarily the non-reciprocal nature of the relation. We can begin by exploring again the metaphor of the face, examined in *Totality and Infinity* as the way in which the other overflows one's own grasping of what the other is. The face, then, describes the phenomenality of the other yet at the same time the very inadequacy of the concept of phenomenality as a way of expressing the other's manifestation. It is not as if the appearance of the other and its excessive presentation were separate things, as if the other were merely unfamiliar but, with time, graspable. Rather, the excessive character of the 'presentation' of the other is the face itself. Yet whether Levinas's assertion that the face of the other is 'the very collapse of phenomenality' or a 'non-phenomenon'[131] is enough to address the concern over his eidetic method is, of course, questionable.

The excessiveness, or height, of the other issues its ethical provocation. Returning for a moment to the idea of the dwelling, the face has the ability to challenge the subject's possession.[132] If the home adorned with possessions is ontology, a position where the world appears for the being, as if the latter were the world's centre, then the encounter with the infinitely other shatters the complacency and apparent legitimacy of this possession. The other eludes the murderous grasp of the being and commands peace. Transcendence is 'stronger than murder'[133] – this strength is derived not from an equivalent, yet greater, strength to that of the being, as if the encounter with the other was a fight over possessions. Instead, the strength that that other manifests is paradoxically derived from its nudity and fragility, its lack of ontological clothing that would allow the being to grapple with it.[134] An attempted murder of the other may flail at its target, but it will never be grasped. The asymmetry of obligation is explicit. It is not as if one can settle the score of ethics, discharging it as if it were a contract. On the contrary, the more that the subject gestures towards the other in responsibility, the more responsible it becomes.[135] Responsibility is infinite.

Totality and Infinity also tells us how the other presents as a 'master' or 'teacher', and how discourse with the other underwrites truth and critical knowledge. The encounter with the other is the means by which the idea of infinity is produced in the subject, which in turn is 'to be taught', in a relation that 'founds Reason'.[136] The expression of the other, in the face of the other, is pure expression. That is, 'expression does not manifest the presence of being by referring from the sign to the signified; it presents the signifier'.[137] This expression, which prompts entry into a relation of teaching (equally described as 'ethical')[138] does not merely refer to a term held in common language, for this would not be teaching. For Levinas, reason, objectivity, truth, and so on – all things that one would think require a closed linguistic system to hold meaning – are in fact preceded by the originary meaning derived from the expression or signification of the other. Likewise, in ethical experience the other is not comprehended with reference to a pre-existent objectivity, but itself founds objectivity. Levinas's critique of ontology does not therefore denounce knowledge, but argues that the 'critical essence' of knowledge is produced in the ethical relation.[139]

The notion of apology is another theme through which the unequal relation with the other operates. Recalling that the other puts the being's possession into question, Levinas similarly characterises this experience as shameful and demanding of atonement. To have is to be exposed to the contestation of one's possession, to experience the injunction to give. Levinas explains that this apologetic gesture is an element of language.[140] The apology seeks judgment, but it is not the brutal and impersonal order of history that will judge,[141] but it is God, infinity itself.[142] Akin to the more developed theme in *Otherwise than Being*, this judgment summons the subject to respond, to be responsible. What is demanded by judgment is infinite responsibility, whose response is the condition for the production of truth and justice, and whose work is inexorable. The response is not a finite punishment, which could be exercised through measure and calculation, but is an infinite duty.[143]

If apology represents an imperative to respond, equivalence is found in *Otherwise than Being* in the shape of the subject's obsession with, and persecution by, the other. These themes allow an understanding of the traumatic nature of the relation with the other. The manner in which the ethical binding to the other arises prior to knowledge and consciousness is characterised by Levinas as obsession.[144] In further conceptual linkage,

Levinas tells us that obsession is persecution, where the relation with the other never has the security of knowledge.[145] The subject is affected and drawn into responsibility for the other who has already passed. This persecution undermines the very knowledge of self and calls the autonomous at-home-with-itself of the subject into question. Thus one should understand persecution in conjunction with the accusation that the other issues. One is called into question, where the accusation being issued is from a time that negates the usual logic of being able to account for and acquit oneself.

If the other obsesses and persecutes, would it not provoke the subject to draw in on itself in an assumption of autonomy antithetical to everything already discussed about Levinasian subjectivity? On the contrary, the effect of persecution is to provoke the subject into taking 'responsibility for the persecutor, and, in this sense from suffering to expiation for the other'.[146] The challenge of passivity is the endurance of passivity through persecution, the seeing of persecution through to the end. It is to seek, impossibly, to make amends for what one is accused of.

This difficult relation is posed as the other holding the subject hostage. This metaphor allows the reader to understand further the implications of Levinasian subjectivity for ideas of freedom. Hostage seems like an evocative state of non-freedom: one is submitted and subjected to another in a manner precisely consistent with the Levinasian subject born into or out of responsibility. Yet if the nature of subjectivity is to be subjected in this manner, it allows one to reconsider the superficial assumption that a characteristic of being hostage is the absence of freedom and that, conversely, freedom is to be found in autonomy. The effect of the other originates from a time that preceded even the question of the subject's freedom. It cannot, except superficially, be thought of as a denial of freedom, and instead opens the very idea of freedom onto a beyond that transcends the limits of autonomy itself.

Zionism

As a postscript to this chapter, it is worth reflecting briefly on another significant branch of Levinas's writings which has yet to be discussed directly. In addition to his scholarly philosophical work, Levinas was an accomplished Talmudic commentator and also wrote many journalistic pieces on Judaism. Some of these writings see Levinas link the broad theme of his ethics to Judaic thinking and practice, whilst another recurring theme – featuring heavily in writings of the 1950s and 1960s – is to consider the political and religious status of Jewish people in the wake of European Nazism and the subsequent establishment of the state of Israel. Commentators on Levinas are split between those who choose to read Levinas's political and theological positions into his philosophy, and those who either see little value in doing so, or believe there is an active risk in pursuing this linkage.[147]

Let us consider, briefly, a couple of his Judaic writings by way of illustration. In an essay entitled 'A Religion for Adults' Levinas talks of the ethical relation being a religious relation, talking of the way in which the arbitrary freedom of the self renders an unintended violence upon the other, linking this to a relationship with God. It is precisely through the relationship provoked by the other that one relates to the divine. Similarly, in 'Jewish Thought Today' he repeats this link, stating that '[e]thics is an optics of the Divine', and that '[t]he Divine can be manifested only through my neighbour'.[148] This form of ethics is crucial to his Judaism, because there is no direct line between the individual and God – it is only through others that the spiritual connection can take place. This ensures that Judaism must always address the political, because spiritual life cannot exist above and beyond the work of politics. Instead, it is rooted in our everyday actions and interrelations with other people. Thus the operation of the state requires that 'the divine word enters into it'.[149] Levinas talks of a messianic state, one that operates as an intermediary stage between the purely earthly realm of idolatry and corruption on the one hand, and on the other the promise of some form of future world outside of history, in which there is abundant peace.

Levinas was always very direct in his Zionism: the messianic state, the state that holds the immeasurable ethical burden of instituting the divine on Earth, is the state of Israel. He was aware that such a notion may be perceived by many as unjustifiable,[150] but was happy to write such claims as '[t]he Messiah institutes a just society and sets humanity free after setting Israel free'.[151] If such writings suggest that the Jews are a chosen people, Levinas is at pains to emphasise that this is not a 'sign of pride' or of entitlement, but instead signifies the way in which responsibility is felt as a singular rather than a general source of duty – a crucial aspect of the ethical structure of subjectivity.[152] This correspondence of the ethical subject and the ethical state is further pronounced when Levinas explains that both evoke a sense of being elected to responsibility, the messianism of which stands to be lost without Israel.[153] The role of Israel here is uniting 'universal history' with a 'particularist messianism'.[154] This interplay of universal and particular is what allows Levinas to explain why the responsibility of Judaic thinking extends beyond just the Jews.

By claiming that truth can be accessed by all, as can religion, Judaism 'aspires' to a universalism, but does so through the particular site of Israel. Responsibility is always felt as unique, and for Judaism Israel is the unique locus of messianic politics.

How should these writings condition our reading of Levinas in this book? It is hopefully not too crude to argue that his philosophical work is sufficiently rich in ideas and free of spiritual baggage, and his political writings sufficiently problematic, to answer: not too much. Whilst his philosophy can be read through his theology, and vice versa, there is little to suggest that this adds anything to the core of his thesis on the nature of subjectivity, time, language, and so on. It is enough to understand that the other represents a transcendent ethical provocation; it is not necessary to go further and perceive the transcendent as a Judeo-Christian God. The extent to which theological terminology plays a narrow analytic role in Levinas's philosophical writings is exemplified in *Totality and Infinity*, where he proposes to 'call "religion" the bond that is established between the same and the other without constituting a totality'.[155] Is there a substantial difference between this designation of 'religion' on the one hand, and, say, the language of poststructuralism on the other? For Levinas, religion provides a certain type of vocabulary that is useful, or at the very least useful to Levinas himself, in working through philosophical ideas that break with the tradition one could call 'Greek', and to open onto questions of the transcendent. But he was explicit about the separability of his religious and philosophical writings. As he made clear in a 1986 interview, 'I keep the two orders separate', he said, affirming his interviewer's suggestion that one can absorb his philosophical insight whilst being completely foreign to the Jewish tradition.[156] In a further interview in the same year, he spoke even more unequivocally of their 'very radical distinction'.[157]

There are even more compelling reasons to be wary of Levinas's position on Israel. Whilst many of his Zionist writings were published when the state of Israel was young, and had yet to assert itself as a nuclear military superpower, it becomes an almost futile effort to read them outside of that context now. Levinas himself wrote of both Israel as a concept and the existent Israel of world history, but if anything, the extent to which such a distinction must be laboured emphasises the difficulty of talking of one without the other.[158] If it is difficult to recognise the universalistic messianism of Levinas's earlier writings in the Israel of today, one can perhaps be forgiving of their earnest and hopeful quality which, with the benefit of hindsight, seems misplaced. Yet this leaves an unavoidable question as to how we interpret Levinas's later hesitance about condemning the apparently Israeli-sanctioned massacre of Palestinian refugees in Lebanon in 1982. '[I]n alterity we can find an enemy,' he said of the question of the Palestinians' otherness, adding, '[t]here are people who are wrong'.[159] It is certainly possible that Levinas here was merely articulating the limits of political and juridical hospitality (as opposed to the unconditionality of ethics), and the difficulty of transposing a descriptive aspect of ethical subjectivity into a normative, political imperative. But it is hard to avoid entirely the feeling that his position in this interview was the result of an enduring commitment to the especial role of Israel in world history, and one which therefore cannot be separated from a critical reading of Zionism that is necessary in the wake of the state-sponsored killing we have become accustomed to seeing in the Middle East. Insensitivity, and this term is without doubt generous, to particular manifestations of otherness punctuate – albeit infrequently – other pieces of his. When writing on the events that condition Jewish thinking of the time (the early 1960s), he warned of the arrival of 'underdeveloped Afro-Asiatic masses' who threaten the Judeo-Christian tradition.[160] Charting Levinas's irregular, ignoble proclivity for occasional racist language, Howard Caygill highlights an even bolder statement of Levinas's anxiety over the alterity of Asia. 'The yellow peril!' Levinas exclaimed, talking of a 'radical strangeness' of Asian populations who are absent from the privileged history of Europe.[161] Can one reconcile such statements with Levinas's claim, elsewhere, that hospitality towards the foreigner 'is a song to the glory of the God of Israel'?[162] Not without difficulty.

Notes

1. Levinas, *Totality and Infinity*, p. 43.
2. A recent study that foregrounds the darker themes of Levinas's work is Sparrow, *Levinas Unhinged*.
3. Levinas, 'Humanism and An-archy', p. 45.
4. Ibid., p. 48. Note that this essay was initially published in 1968, a time at which the likes of Foucault and Lévi-Strauss were flourishing within the French intellectual scene. For an extended study of Levinas's relationship with humanism and anti-humanism, see Sederberg, 'Resaying the Human'.
5. For a discussion of this feature of Levinas's outlook, see Critchley, 'Prolegomena to Any Post-Deconstructive Subjectivity'. More generally, see Cadava et al., *Who Comes After the Subject?*.
6. Malka, *Emmanuel Levinas*, p. 35.

7. Husserl, *Logical Investigations Volume 1*, p. 168.
8. Husserl, *Cartesian Meditations*, p. 21.
9. Levinas, 'Philosophy and Awakening', p. 209.
10. Derrida, 'Violence and Metaphysics', p. 108.
11. Ibid.
12. Heidegger, *Being and Time*, p. 26.
13. Ibid., p. 34.
14. Ibid., p. 27.
15. Ibid., p. 39.
16. Here we can note that the question of being is informed by the temporality of concealment and revelation. Unlike in Hegel, this is a question that cannot be contained within dialectic certainty; it must address that which has been 'concealed', which informs Being without presenting itself on the ontic level. It is, arguably, this importance of the concealed or the 'unthought' that situates difference in Heidegger's thought. This leads Mark C. Taylor to make the following interpretation: 'In attempting to think what philosophy leaves unthought, Heidegger discovers a difference that cannot be reduced to identity. This difference is an other that can never be named properly' (Taylor, *Altarity*, p. 52). Thus, if we accept this position, the 'subject' – the Dasein that is always asking the question of its own being – is inextricably linked to and determined by alterity. This, one might argue, is a generous or at least uncritical reading of Heidegger, certainly with respect to the critique levelled by Levinas.
17. Levinas, 'Martin Heidegger and Ontology', p. 16.
18. As noted in Committee of Public Safety, 'Reflections on the Thought of Emmanuel Levinas', p. 6.
19. Levinas, *On Escape*, p. 49.
20. Ibid., p. 50.
21. Ibid., p. 66.
22. Ibid., p. 51.
23. Ibid., p. 54.
24. Ibid., p. 69.
25. Ibid., p. 55. Original emphasis removed.
26. The French title is *De l'existence à l'existant*, making a more literal translation '*From* Existence *to* Existents.'
27. Levinas, *Existence and Existents*, p. 9.
28. Ibid., p. 12.
29. Ibid., p. 15.

30. Ibid., p. 20.
31. Levinas, 'Martin Heidegger and Ontology', p. 20.
32. Ibid.
33. Levinas, *Existence and Existents*, p. 34.
34. Ibid., p. 36.
35. Ibid., p. 37.
36. Ibid., p. 52.
37. Ibid.
38. Ibid., p. 55.
39. Ibid., p. 52.
40. Ibid. Insomnia is a metaphor that appears in the early post-war writings of Levinas, but also appears in some of his much later pieces, such as the essay 'God and Philosophy' (see Levinas, *Of God Who Comes to Mind*, pp. 58–9).
41. Levinas, *Existence and Existents*, p. 61.
42. Heidegger, *Being and Time*, p. 356.
43. Levinas, *Existence and Existents*, p. 58.
44. Rolland, 'Getting Out of Being by a New Path', p. 43.
45. Levinas, *Existence and Existents*, p. 69.
46. Ibid., p. 70.
47. Levinas, *Time and the Other*, p. 52.
48. Levinas, *Existence and Existents*, p. 76.
49. Ibid., p. 84.
50. Levinas, *On Escape*, p. 55.
51. Levinas, *Otherwise than Being*, p. 124.
52. Levinas, *Existence and Existents*, p. 96.
53. Levinas, *Time and the Other*, p. 72.
54. Ibid., p. 74.
55. See Levinas, *Entre Nous*, pp. 1–10.
56. Ibid., p. 7.
57. Ibid.
58. Derrida, 'Violence and Metaphysics', p. 100. Incidentally, Derrida's rhetorical question of 'Are we Jews? Are we Greeks?' in the same piece (p. 191) is the source of this subsection's title.
59. Ibid.
60. Levinas, *Alterity and Transcendence*, pp. 8–9.
61. Derrida, 'Violence and Metaphysics', p. 104.
62. Levinas, *Totality and Infinity*, p. 21.
63. Ibid.
64. Ibid., pp. 22–3.

65. Ibid., p. 23.
66. Ibid., p. 26.
67. Ibid., p. 53.
68. Levinas, *Entre Nous*, p. 169.
69. Derrida embeds his potent critique in consistently generous and polite terms (for example, it is suggested that very the radical nature of Levinas's thought might make us 'tremble' (p. 103) and *Totality and Infinity* is more than once described as a 'great work'). It has also been suggested that Derrida does not issue a criticism as such, but simply explains how metaphysics can be disrupted from within its own language. See Cornell, 'Post-Structuralism, the Ethical Relation, and the Law'.
70. Derrida, 'Violence and Metaphysics', p. 110.
71. Levinas, *Totality and Infinity*, pp. 261–2.
72. Derrida, 'Violence and Metaphysics', pp. 139–40.
73. Bergo, *Levinas Between Ethics and Politics*, p. 133.
74. Ibid., p. 134. The work by Strasser that Bergo paraphrases is *Jenseits von Sein und Zeit*.
75. Peperzak, *To the Other*, p. 217, quoted in Bergo, *Levinas Between Ethics and Politics*, pp. 145–6.
76. Levinas, *Otherwise than Being*, p. xlvii.
77. Ibid., p. 4.
78. Ibid., pp. 4–5.
79. Ibid., p. 3.
80. Ibid., p. 29.
81. Ricoeur, 'Otherwise', p. 82.
82. Levinas, *Otherwise than Being*, p. 34.
83. Ibid., p. 37.
84. Ibid., p. 43.
85. Ibid., p. 45.
86. Ibid., p. 46.
87. Ibid., p. 47.
88. Ibid., p. 25.
89. See Ricoeur, 'Otherwise', p. 86.
90. Levinas, *Totality and Infinity*, p. 55.
91. Ibid., p. 60.
92. Ibid., p. 114.
93. Ibid., p. 115.
94. Ibid., p. 110.
95. Ibid., p. 117.

96. Ibid., pp. 148–9.
97. Ibid., p. 158.
98. Ibid., p. 155.
99. Ibid., p. 156.
100. The ethical dilemma here is evoked by Levinas's well known prefacing of *Otherwise than Being* with a quote from Pascal: "'That is my place in the sun." That is how the usurpation of the world began' (Levinas, *Otherwise than Being*, p. vii).
101. Levinas, *Totality and Infinity*, p. 171.
102. The 'pre-ethical' nature of this welcome is a phrase coined by Derrida in *Adieu*, pp. 38–9.
103. Levinas, *Otherwise than Being*, p. 47.
104. Ibid., p. 91.
105. Ibid., p. 49.
106. Ibid., p. 55.
107. Ibid., p. 66.
108. Ibid., p. 68.
109. Ibid., p. 81.
110. Ibid., p. 82. Author's emphasis.
111. Ibid., p. 90.
112. Levinas, *Of God Who Comes to Mind*, pp. 13–14.
113. Levinas, *Otherwise than Being*, p. 85.
114. Ibid., p. 101.
115. Ibid., p. 104.
116. Ibid., pp. 102–9.
117. Ibid., p. 114.
118. Ibid., p. 115.
119. Ibid., p. 124.
120. On the relation between the themes of escape and substitution, see Diamantides, 'From Escape to Hostage'. As Diamantides puts it, hostage is characterised by its impossibility, that it operates as 'an aspiration - not a fact', meaning that we are never truly substituted; ultimately, we always remain bound to ourselves (p. 197).
121. Levinas, *Otherwise than Being*, p. 127.
122. Levinas, *Totality and Infinity*, p. 224.
123. Ibid., p. 233.
124. Ibid., p. 230.
125. Ibid., p. 236.
126. Ibid., p. 284.
127. Ibid., p. 284.

128. Levinas, *Otherwise than Being*, p. 88.
129. Ibid.
130. Ibid., p. 89.
131. Ibid., p. 88.
132. Levinas, *Totality and Infinity*, p. 171.
133. Ibid., p. 199.
134. Ibid., pp. 199–200.
135. Levinas, *Otherwise than Being*, p. 93; *Totality and Infinity*, p. 244.
136. Levinas, *Totality and Infinity*, p. 204.
137. Ibid., pp. 181–2.
138. Ibid., p. 181.
139. Ibid., p. 43.
140. Ibid., p. 252.
141. Ibid., p. 242.
142. Ibid., p. 244.
143. Ibid.
144. Levinas, *Otherwise than Being*., p. 101.
145. Ibid.
146. Ibid., p. 111.
147. For an example of work that seeks to link Levinas's religious and philosophical views, see Gibbs, *Correlations in Rosenzweig and Levinas*; and on the subject of law, see Gibbs, 'Law and Ethics.' Also see Stone, *Reading Levinas/Reading Talmud*. For an essay warning of the dangers of reading Levinas's work too closely to a Judaic religious and political tradition, see Critchley, 'Five Problems in Levinas's View of Politics'.
148. Levinas, *Difficult Freedom*, p. 159.
149 Levinas, *Beyond the Verse*, p. 174.
150. Levinas, *Difficult Freedom*, p. 216.
151. Levinas, *Beyond the Verse*, p. 174
152. Levinas, *Difficult Freedom*, p. 176.
153. Ibid., p. 96.
154. Ibid.
155. Levinas, *Totality and Infinity*, p. 40.
156. Levinas, *Is It Righteous to Be?*, p. 62.
157. The clear distinction between these two branches of writings was the subject of Levinas's answer when prompted in a 1986 interview to comment on the extent to which they could be read independently of each other. Levinas even goes as far as making a point of

the fact that they had different publishers (Levinas, 'The Paradox of Morality', p. 173).

158. Simon Critchley has written specifically on the problematic of Israel getting stuck in this tension between its ideal and embodied political existence in Levinas's work (Critchley, 'Five Problems').

159. Levinas, 'Ethics and Politics', p. 294.

160. Levinas, *Difficult Freedom*, p. 160.

161. Levinas, *Les imprevus de l'histoire*, p. 172, quoted in Caygill, *Levinas and the Political*, p. 184.

162. Levinas, *In the Time of the Nations*, p. 86. See also Derrida's discussion of this passage, in which he lends a (somewhat charitable) reading of a universally human gesture of hospitality that is opened by Israel's election to hospitality towards its outsiders (Derrida, *Adieu*, p. 72).

Part II
Ethics and Law

3

Can Law Be Ethical?

Ethics and Justice

Moving from the ethical to the legal (or, indeed, the political) is an irreducible problem within the Levinasian framework. This is not an internal failing of his thought. Were it not a problem, were there an easy solution to this relationship, Levinas's ethics would of course lose all of their radical purchase. Ethics is, by definition, a unique relationship. It is the very singularity of subjectivity put into discord with the infinitely chasmic accusation by the other that constitutes not only ethics but the very movement of subjectivity. The question is how we move from the singular to the general, from the personal to the juridical, from the one-to-one to the multiplicity? The singular nature of Levinas's ethics inevitably poses a challenge for any form of legal signification. This chapter will consider a number of possible answers to this question. Firstly, it will examine Levinas's own somewhat brief meditations on the passage from ethics to law via his conception of justice.

Totality and Infinity hints at ideas he would develop further later on but stops short of providing a convincing answer to this problem. Firstly (and with a consistently problematic gender politics in evidence), he claims that ethical subjectivity is experienced in fraternity. The peculiar structure of ethical election recalls Levinas's favoured excerpt from Dostoevsky's *The Brothers Karamazov*: 'Each of us is guilty before everyone and for everything, and I more than all the others'.[1] The call to responsibility is felt as if only I can answer it, as an accusation that strikes to the heart of me alone. But it is an injunction that is addressed to every individual as an equal, each person being irreplaceably unique.[2] To be an ethical subject is to be so alongside other ethical subjects (specifically brothers, to use the fraternal metaphor). Levinas makes it clear that fraternity is not the result of ethical obligation, as if brotherhood were merely the consequence of a shared ethical disposition. Rather, the very possibility of facing the other is conditioned by fraternity: the face manifests because it belongs to a brother, not vice versa. Therefore every ethical relation refers to the social as a whole, despite its own singularity. Dialogue addressed to the other does not operate in a vacuum, and is also referred to all the other others, the figurative 'third party' that would take on a more central position in his later writings. The picture that Levinas paints of the social existence of ethics is, therefore, one of solidarity. The fraternity of this social bond constitutes a 'We'.[3]

Insofar as one can draw a politics from *Totality and Infinity*, its political aspirations are gathered around the idea of messianic time, a horizon of time that promises its completion in 'pure triumph'.[4] This eschatological thematic signals one particular dimension of Levinas's political thinking, the way that a politics of futurity issues a questioning of the ontological formation of the state and its institutions. Nevertheless, Levinas did turn his attention to the problem of ethics in a social collective in the form of a more grounded set of questions: this ethical responsiveness 'moves into the form of a We, aspires to a State, institutions, laws, which are the source of universality'.[5] This unicity does not find its final accomplishment in the state, however. The juridical form of law and politics can never arrive at a full expression of ethics – insofar as its universality asserts a totality, ethics must maintain a perpetual challenge upon the state. In this regard, one can see the crucial significance of the seemingly modest idea of 'aspiration' in the above passage. Ethics cannot do more than simply aspire to be embodied in the state, as the relation between state and ethics is one of aporia. Ethics need laws and political structures to be expressed in the social, yet such apparatuses will always necessarily fail ethics by reducing the signification of transcendence to totality, the otherwise than being into essence.

Levinas's position is developed further in his later works, when he considers the tension between singularity and universality as a more distinct problematic of judgment. What happens to ethical duties when, after the emergence of subjectivity in its 'finite freedom', it is *forced* to choose? Ethics determines the subject, but upon its emergence the subject finds itself in a world surrounded by others and therefore faced with dilemmas. The multiplicity, the more than two, is signified by what Levinas again calls 'the third', not in the sense of the literal interruption of the one-to-one ethical encounter by another empirical person's arrival, but as a signifier for the irreducible presence of the other others and the necessity of the language of the said. It is the third that indicates the immediacy of 'the question', not merely of '[w]hy philosophy',[6] or why institute an ontological structure that allows us to know. It is also the very question of the question, of how we can make judgments, and how we can decide. If the relationship remained limited merely between the subject and the other, then no question would ever arise, and no decision would have to be made. This intimacy of the one-to-one only becomes problematised by the third who disrupts the ethical relation, demanding attention and distancing the subject from the other.[7]

How does one answer the question that arises in the presence of the third? The question demands

> comparison, coexistence, contemporaneousness, assembling, order, thematization, the visibility of faces, and thus intentionality and the intellect, and in intentionality and the intellect the intelligibility of a system, and thence also a copresence on an equal footing as before a court of justice.[8]

In a brief passage from the 1984 essay 'Peace and Proximity' he is even more direct. The demands of justice call for 'the political structure of society under the rule of law' and an institutional framework to reflect a 'perfect reciprocity of political laws that are essentially egalitarian or held to be so'.[9]

The necessary appearance of the third therefore demands comparing, ranking and deciding between incommensurable demands by assimilating them within a coherent thematic framework. It requires that the subject shares, and thus measures, its attention in distinction to the infinite and singular attention that ethics requires. The third represents another other, yet opens the possibility that each might be the 'persecutor' of the other one.[10] The ethical obligations that one is placed under demand choice, and to choose requires the intelligibility of a common language, a said, something that may allow translation between alien demands and allow the choice to become coherent. This return to the said is justice itself, a principle or law that undermines the radical ethical relation, yet which is absolutely necessary if law seeks to articulate our responsibilities to each other, however imperfectly. Justice therefore requires the reduction of the other to the same, traversing the chasm between the proximity of the other and the totality of law and politics. Whilst Levinas characterises the work of justice as, to some extent, a 'betrayal' of the other and its anarchic call,[11] it also has the effect of cementing a social bond. Through the presence of the third and the exigency of justice, the I is not just an ethical subject but also an other for all the other others, and is therefore accounted for in the structures of law and politics that arise out of justice's demands. As William Simmons emphasises, the political or legal responsibility felt in the presence of the third must be understood very differently to the ethical responsibility provoked by the other: where the latter is singular and infinite, the former is both measured and capable of universalisation amongst all people within a representable principle.[12]

Thus whilst the proximal relation with the other is compromised, the subjectivity that is provoked by the third still owes itself to the ethical relation. When Levinas says '[t]he foundation of consciousness is justice'[13] he means the necessity for drawing inward into the fixity of the said and of synchrony is precisely the third's presence, the facticity of society, and the demand for justice (albeit not necessarily limited to juridical justice). It has already been explained that subjectivity in Levinas is in torsion and anguish, burdened with its-self and responsible for the other. The side of this torsion that pulls the subject inward, the side of the said and of synchrony, arises with the third party. We can therefore understand Levinas's striking claim that 'there is question [sic] of the said and being only because saying or responsibility require justice'.[14] This is a crucial insight, as it emphasises justice as the link between saying and said. Through justice, the said is the social vehicle of the saying. When there are more than two interlocutors, ethics needs law and politics to provide it with a voice. Likewise, the state needs ethics if it is to have a worthy direction, and avoid being simply a game of power and bureaucracy within an ontological totality.[15]

The gap between these two orders, ethics on the one hand and the ontological realm of the juridical/political on the other, is described by Simon Critchley as a 'hiatus'.[16] This observation rightly invokes an irreducible gap, the aporia of the undecidable, which disallows a calculable deduction from one to the other. The common intelligibility of the said might give the decision a cognitive rationale, but this is not determined by the saying. One still has to traverse the hiatus. Louis Wolcher frames the same problem in a slightly different, but equally compelling manner, asking how the subject can know what justice entails if the preceding order of ethics escapes its ontological graspability. Moreover, how does the subject survive this passage, unconditionally bonded to the other in one (ethical) moment, and required to justify its (legal) judgment the next?[17] Levinas himself does not provide us with a direct answer to these questions. We could, of course, attribute this to the essential characteristic of aporia. As Derrida would remind us, the decision is mad, and we cannot deploy an ethical justification of a legal decision. Ethical provocation is what puts justice at stake in the legal decision in front of us, but it does not tell us what to decide. Nevertheless, as we shall see, the 'problem of passage' as Wolcher dubs it will continually (de)limit the direct application of this ethical philosophy to questions of law.

We can, at this point, make a couple of initial observations about these brief references to law. First, justice for Levinas takes on an adjudicative form. Law can arise out of the demands of justice, and justice is achieved through qualities we naturally associate with law in modern Western society: the mediation of disputes, the comparing and ranking of the priority of parties' demands, a concern for equality and 'equity'[18] between parties, and so on. Furthermore, despite its radicalised understanding of alterity, it contorts and reimagines elements of a distinctly liberal jurisprudence, one which is constituted in the superimposition of formal equality and reciprocity over the radical singularity of ethics. Secondly, justice is of an order that is not itself an ethics. There is a gap between the two that ensures that justice is never just enough. It is always marked by some extent of failure, in that it erases the signification of the other in the very gesture that seeks to transpose the ethical into the legal. In this sense, we can understand Levinas's comment that whilst it is necessary, still 'there is a violence in justice'.[19] Thirdly, Levinas's undeveloped view of law is often conflated with politics, and reflects an arguably naïve (or more charitably, utopian) view of our capacity to incorporate disparate demands into a coherent whole. For instance, in speaking of the demands of justice he talks in 'Peace and Proximity' of 'the necessity of thinking together beneath one synthetic theme the multiple and the unity of the world'.[20]

The remainder of the chapter considers three different, although not necessarily mutually exclusive, approaches to incorporating Levinas's ethics into a concept of law and its processes. First, it will begin to develop an understanding of the relationship between law and ontology, utilising Levinas's ideas on justice whilst furthermore placing them into dialogue with his broader ideas on temporality. The idea of legal ontology will be taken up further in the latter section of the book. Secondly, it asks to what extent ethical responsibility might be identified within the content of legal norms. In other words, in addition to explicating the dilemma of justice that one locates in processes of adjudication, can the proximal ethical bond also determine the way we fill out the substance of law in a way that reflects our fundamental duties towards each other as part of a political community? Lastly, the chapter will examine a much more cautious, perhaps pessimistic, alternative that suggests that his philosophy is better mobilised as a framework for critiquing or attacking the dominant legal form. Levinas's writings on the an-archic quality of ethics will be the especial subject of focus here.

Law, Language and Time – Towards a Legal Ontology

Levinas's concept of the third, summarised above, represents his most considered reflection on law, but he fails to develop it beyond the issue he considers most important in these passages, which is how the saying can find a trace of distorted expression in the said, and how consciousness and essence emerge out of the antecedent responsibility for the other. It presents us with a crucial but limited account of law, which is how law can be constituted in response to, but not reducible to, ethics. It should be clear from Levinas's writing that he did not intend to claim that law is always an expression of justice. This is not only apparent in his various warnings about state institutions that abandon ethical reflection ('[p]olitics left to itself bears a tyranny within itself',[21] for example) but is also the only tenable interpretation of his application to grounded legal practices. Whilst subjectivity is born out of a constitutive ethical debt to others, there is no guarantee that this always filters into our institutions and our shared ontology. Justice is difficult, where a mundane deference to the said is easy. Justice is irruptive and exceptional; it must alternate between breaking up, rewriting and justifying its principles,[22] whilst examples of legal processes that merely perpetuate the totality of the same are innumerable. Levinas's description of the disruptive exigency of the other and the third is hard to imagine in, for instance, a tenant seeking arbitration of a deposit dispute with their landlord, or a ruling determining a person's tax payable on their estate, or delineating a local authority's powers to set parking restrictions. Indeed, even in the most dramatic process of law, the trial, a technical application of precedent may leave limited room for the exceptional demand of ethics. This subsection takes up the task of extending Levinas's references to law, in order to think more comprehensively about the circumstances in which a legal decision can be 'just' in the Levinasian sense and, moreover, the ways in which law has a foundationally ontological character. Primarily, we need to tie Levinas's references to law more closely to his extensive and rigorous analyses of language and time.

It is first necessary to consider how law corresponds to Levinas's pairing of synchrony and diachrony. Law cannot be understood effectively without a notion of temporality.[23] The application of precedent is a process that both looks to the past as a source of wisdom, but lives in the present by trying to construct a model of what the law *is* through its history. Judgment operates in the present by making claims about the past, whilst at the same time, law-making always anticipates the future. The linearity of conventional law-time means that it both presumes and entrenches a correspondence of past, present and future, in a manner that is inseparable from the dominance of linear conceptions of time in modernity.[24] What will be claimed in the following analysis is that law is primarily concerned with the present, and with presencing – but this is precisely the consequence, not the reduction, of law's temporality. It is a fundamental principle of legal reasoning that law is not capricious or retroactive, and that therefore one's role is to interpret and apply law, and leave the overt creation of new law to policymakers and revolutionaries. This is not to assume, naively, that legal reasoning is always mechanical, but rather to emphasise that even acts of judicial creativity do not arise spontaneously, and even in the most activist contexts derive – in part – from some sense of obligation towards the past as well as foresight of the future.

An act of legal judgment is a temporally-determined statement of, or claim to, the law's being. Here, 'law's being' refers not merely to the presence of law itself, but also law's ontological status as an expression of our shared reality; that is, what is *presented by* law. Law's temporality brings it to presence as a function of its past and its future. It is present, it *is*, because it sustains through time. Costas Douzinas, in his study of time and the law, claims that '[a]bsence, what has been or what is to come, is a manner of presencing'.[25] In other words, the linear past – an absent past present – sustains a presence through the construction of memory and history. Or more specifically, in the case of law and legal reasoning, through *stare decisis*. Whilst Levinas failed to foreground it extensively himself, law is a very good example of the synchronic expression of being, which is not to say that past and future cease to operate upon our understanding of the world, but on the contrary, that synchrony denotes their correspondence, their linear connection with, and constitution of, the present. Of course, we do not have unfiltered access to the past. Quite the opposite, the past is perpetually rewritten and reconstituted in our acts of memory, renewing its link with the now.

A simplistic example of legal reasoning illustrates this. Take a common scenario in which a case law precedent is cited to justify a particular judicial decision, such that there is a relationship between present and past. In Levinasian terms, any legal judgment must involve a saying – in literal terms, it is of course a spoken work of language – but would additionally be what Levinas calls a saying that is correlative with the said.[26] This is a saying that simply reiterates essence, rather than signifying the otherwise-than-being. It makes a claim to law's being, and does so in a way that 'coagulate[s] the flow of time' into determinate meaning.[27] This is not to say we lose sense of the past in the application of case law; on the contrary, the precedent makes sense because it brings meaning to the present/presence of the law through a direct homology. The past becomes present, and law's being sustains through time.[28] In this sense we can understand the law's temporality as synchronic, not in the sense that all times become identical, but in the sense that they are all a function of the present/presence.

Before moving on to consider more complex legal reasoning, it is necessary to say more on not simply the temporal but also the linguistic aspect of law as ontology. The aspect of language focused upon most directly by Levinas is the verb, the exemplary form of which is 'to be', which designates being as an event occurring in time. When turned to law, it might not be immediately apparent how such an analysis of language could be applied. What is the fundamental verb-form of law? We do not say that the law is engaged in acts of 'law-ing'. We might think of the verb 'to judge', but of course it is not the law that judges; law is the interpretive fabric that allows for judgment. Levinas, as if anticipating this, solves the problem by explaining how the noun-form of language cannot be fully distinguished from the verb. In describing what he repeatedly calls the 'amphibology of being and entities', Levinas claims that nouns also, although less obviously, invoke the being that is implied by verbs.[29] To say that 'A is A' is to say 'the A As'; or, to say that something is a 'sound' is to say that 'it resounds'.[30] By invoking this expressive porosity between being and entities, Levinas refutes the idea that language can be cleanly split into static substances and dynamic events. Language as a whole is implicated in the temporality of ontology, in the structure of saying and said. This observation is particularly important, because so much of legal reasoning is designation, nomination and identification. It is a process of establishing correspondence in the same structure of the noun-form, proclaiming, to use a phrase of Levinas, the 'this as that'.[31] For example, ruling that foreseeing the virtually certain consequences of one's actions is 'intention' for the purposes of establishing the *mens rea* of murder in criminal law.[32] Such nomination also expresses a synchronisation, through this amphibology, as it works equivalently to bring to being whatever is nominated. There is, therefore, a specifically ontological significance to the designation of certain types of mental states as criminally culpable.

In addition to presencing the rules and principles of law, legal reasoning makes ontological claims over facts that are necessary for legal judgment. There is no better example of this than the criminal jury trial, in which the task of the laypeople is to determine whether the sequence of past events occurred in the manner put forward by the prosecution, with such certainty that the court can pronounce unequivocally that the defendant is guilty. This inevitably appears as a backwards-looking examination of the past, but it is important to understand how there are gestures of presencing here. First, synchronisation operates through the linear framing of time, between past and present versions of the defendant. An evidential study of past events allows for judgment to make a claim about the defendant's present. Guilt is what constitutes the present legal significance of the defendant out of the past, through a linear function of time. Secondly, it is important to note the well-documented claim that the version of the past verified by the jury's verdict is, like any work of history, constructed. This is not simply because, as noted above, history does not have the privilege of unmediated access to the past (indeed, the idea of a past with which we can engage without filter is mythical). More specifically, the guilty verdict is reached by a jury accepting a narrative presented and brought into presence by the prosecution such that it corresponds with abstract legal rules and principles.[33]

An objection to this form of analysis needs to be dealt with pre-emptively before proceeding further. If ontology is a study of being, how can this argument for thinking law as 'legal ontology' survive if we think of law, as many do, as a framework of norms? Is it not the case that ontology, in Levinas's view, is an expression of what *is*, rather than what ought to be? This is an important question that will be taken up in full in Chapter 5, where the book will analyse the contemporary legal paradigm of liberal biopolitics. This phenomenon, it will be argued, sees legal meaning collapsing into a descriptive schema of knowledge claims. The full extent of this critical argument cannot be drawn out here, but a more fundamental observation can be made with respect to Levinas's view of norms and laws. Whilst not exhaustive of law, justice is the expression of law that seeks to meet the impossible challenge of ethics. But it is absolutely clear that when Levinas remarks, speaking of justice, that the 'saying becomes fixed in a said, is written, becomes a book, law and science',[34] he is referring to the emergence of a graspable, representable order of being – one that allows us to know, to compare and, significantly, to judge. He is making a claim about law's descriptive quality, the way that it allows us to make some shared, thematisable sense of the problem in front of us. Levinas is right in understanding law in this way, and it is not to say we must abandon any notion of normativity in law. Consider a basic example of a legal norm, such as 'you should not take property that does not belong to you'. It is untenable that this norm can operate meaningfully without making an ontological claim about social being. It is to affirm our most fundamental understandings of the individual and their autonomy, and of the sanctity of property in an economic social structure based on exchange. We can certainly justify the law against theft as a norm using moral argumentation, but the way it acts upon people's behaviour in everyday life is built into our understanding of being to the extent that it becomes almost indistinguishable from the most basic frameworks of understanding. It is apt that Levinas would refer to law and science in the same breath – legal ontology has the same character as a law of physics: the nature of legal ontology means it tends towards the instinctive familiarity of a Newtonian principle. But we also have to be careful here not to veer into an argument for legal naturalism. That law has an ontological character is not to say it is immutable, nor that it gains any specific legitimacy from its role in supporting our everyday understanding of being. Indeed, as the latter two chapters of this book will argue, the ontological character of law must be understood critically and in ideological terms.

So far it has been suggested that there is a basic ontological status of legal rules and reasoning. Moving on, an analysis of law's temporality forces us to consider scenarios in which the law is made to change. This is an important problem, because the function of ontological synchronisation is a reduction to sameness. Whilst it allows us to understand how law maintains its façade of coherence and consistency, it might not be readily apparent how it allows law to adapt. In many appellate judgments the synchronic principle continues to apply because although the decision might overrule rather than follow a particular precedent, this may be justified merely by an appeal to an earlier authority. Therefore, the law's being sustains; it was already there to be discovered. But there are instances in which the law adapts in a rather more inventive fashion, which raise further questions as to the operation of time and language. Take *R* v. *R* [1991] 1 AC 599, a famous criminal law appeal to the House of Lords, which had to decide whether the law continued to recognise a marital exemption to the crime of rape, allowing a husband to have non-consensual sex with his wife. That such an exemption existed in the eighteenth century was not disputed. The question was whether it continued to exist and, somewhat more technically, whether its operation was preserved by the new statutory framework governing sexual offences. The

Sexual Offences (Amendment) Act 1976 had defined rape as 'unlawful' non-consensual sexual intercourse. This phrasing led the appellant in the case to argue that the inclusion of the word 'unlawful' implied that lawful non-consensual intercourse must also be possible, indicating that the marital exemption must still exist. Lord Keith spent some time early in his judgment describing the English common law's capacity to evolve and adapt to changing social values and attitudes. Since the first expression of the marital exemption, marriage had changed from a relation of quasi-ownership of wife by husband to a 'partnership of equals', and society would not accept the characterisation of marriage implied by the exemption.[35] Unsurprisingly, the House of Lords decided to reject the appeal and agree with the Court of Appeal that no such marital exemption exists anymore. Having held that the word 'unlawful' was nothing more than surplusage in the drafting of the statute, Lord Keith concluded that 'the Act of 1976 presents no obstacle to this House declaring that in modern times the supposed marital exemption in rape forms no part of the law of England'.[36]

This case is not anomalous, but is simply an extreme demonstration of the irreducible tension within common law jurisprudence, which holds that we must abide by the principles of *stare decisis* whilst at the same time adapting the law in a workable manner. In this case the tension is pronounced, and appears in the very words of the judgment, whereby Lord Keith in one stroke holds that 'it is clearly unlawful to have sexual intercourse with any woman without her consent' and in another approvingly quotes Lord Lane in the Court of Appeal referring to 'the removal of a common law fiction' of the marital exemption.[37] Here, there is slippage between the claim that the House of Lords is simply applying a law that already exists (as implied in the first statement), and the claim that it is an act that positively changes the law by its own performative force (as implied by the second). In other words, the slippage operates between a simple deference to an existing said, and the inventive act in which a legal principle becomes solidified in the said via its reduction from an act of saying. The common law can only subsist in the aporia between the two – it cannot be the pure application of existing law, a perpetual and totalised echoing of the said, but nor can it be pure invention in the form of a judge's absolute freedom to grapple with saying and said in the pursuit of discretionary justice. It is in the creative and responsive moment of saying that law accommodates the possibility of ethics. And it is within this aporia between saying and said that law can do the work of Levinasian justice, giving a judgment on the dignity and coherence of legal rationality whilst accounting for one's ethical responsibility.

Furthermore, the second statement, dismissing the act of invention as the mere removal of an outdated fiction, is something of a fudge, as the marital exemption is of course no more fictitious than any other provision of the common law. It was certainly accepted to be valid law after its eighteenth-century pronouncement. It could of course be inferred from Lord Keith's words that what made it fictitious (and, we are led to believe, of impaired validity) is that it no longer accorded with public approval. This would lead to a rather peculiar conclusion, however, that the law is capable of changing through time without the intervention of any judgment or other interpretative act. On the contrary, unless we are to formulate some sort of dynamic, metaphysical natural law that evolves of its own accord, we must accept that it is the act of judgment that changes the law, actively rendering it an inconvenient fiction purely by constative force.

Peter Fitzpatrick frames the matter as one of origin. To the extent that it is fictive, 'law remains the same whilst it has changed completely,'[38] allowing it to adapt (via what Fitzpatrick terms its responsiveness) yet simultaneously maintaining its fixity through time. Ultimately, this necessitates the malleability of the origin of law, the initial creative act that inaugurates a structure of legal meaning.[39] Being able to re-write the origin, the condition of which is, of course, law's fictive nature, reveals a double temporality in legal reasoning, allowing law to change through time but only by negating the change by inscribing it into a deeper authority – ultimately the origin – that holds that this is how the law has always been. We can, therefore, understand Fitzpatrick's elegant formulation quoted above: law is constantly changing, but only by remaining the same. Meanwhile, in Levinasian terms, the proximity of the other remains *pre-originary*, provoking (but not determining, nor exhausting) the constitution of origins in the difficult movement across the hiatus from ethics to law.[40]

The declaration of a legal principle or rule is an expression of legal essence. It is a (re-)presenting of law's being. This is immediately apparent in the side of the aporia in which legal reasoning appears non-retroactive – it expresses what already exists (and which is manifest in Lord Lane's protestation that the court was not engaged in creating a new rule).[41] As a synchronic expression of the said, it negates diachrony – the otherness of times to each other – giving the law a presence whereby past, present and future are constitutively connected, and effacing the spontaneity of pure invention. In this manner, the law of rape as re-presented in *R* v. *R* signals no diachronic break with the past. The law has changed whilst remaining an order of the same; any disjuncture in this change is hidden in the judgment, which instead justifies the decision through a construction of what the law is.

Law may or may not be 'just' in the Levinasian sense. The question depends on the extent to which the reproduction of law's being springs from the temporalisation of the diachronic provocation of the other into the synchronic form of the said,[42] or whether, on the contrary, it merely echoes law's uninterrupted presence. Looking for traces of justice in legal judgments is, to a large extent, folly. As the discussion of *R* v. *R* has sought to show, the nature of legal reasoning is to cover up the original diastasis that provoked the synchronic process of justice. It is not hard to imagine this judgment emerging out of the difficult passage from uniquely felt responsibility into the abstract weighing-up of egalitarian and just legal principle. Yet it might also simply be the product of, on the contrary, what Levinas called the 'anonymous legality' of a 'technique of social equilibrium';[43] in other words, law reproducing itself for the sake of law, without the interruptive shock of the other's pre-ontological provocation. There is nothing necessarily malign in the latter, but it is quite different from what Levinas described as justice. The 'problem of passage' ensures that philosophising is unlikely to tell us, in any given case, whether its judgment originated in the same or the other.

Ethics in Legal Norms

Where the previous section considered the dynamics of being within institutional processes of law, we can now move to think about whether the very content of law could have, or even should have, an ethical basis. This question is somewhat distinct, asking not merely of the ways in which ethics provokes law to respond justly to the other(s) within adjudication, but also of the way law may command each of us to follow the injunction of ethics in relation to each other, irrespective of being party to any sort of dispute. What would it mean for law to try to make us act ethically?

This section will not dwell on the existing, well-known discussions within Anglo-American jurisprudence about whether a moral dimension of law is necessary for that law to be valid. Levinas's conception of ethics is both more complex and more nebulous than the narrower ideas of morals associated with orthodox legal theory (which tend to be pervasively conservative, or assimilative in their purported reflection of common standards within a community, or simply under-theorised). The principal problem of transposing the ethical idea of responsibility to the other into a legal norm is that, as discussed earlier, the two are of entirely different orders, one unconditional, singular, pre-reflective, the other objective, universal and justifiable. In her exploration of whether Levinasian ethics 'can generate norms', Diane Perpich rightly notes the way that Levinas therefore presents a theory about ethics, not a norma-tive theory of what is substantively ethical. She is right when she boldly surmises that Levinas's work 'does not provide a principle or algorithm that could be used to determine the rightness or wrongness of some given action'.[44] In a similar vein, Devorah Wainer has put forward a compelling argument that Levinas forces us to confront the very limits of thinking of responsibility. It is not merely that Levinas omits to provide a concrete normative framework, but also that he should not be read as granting a 'theory' of how we act with respect to the other at all – certainly not to the extent that one can generate determinate policy ideas.[45]

Further, there are those who might see a supreme weakness in Levinas's thought on precisely this issue. Gillian Rose has levelled a powerful attack on Levinas's political philosophy, articulated most comprehensively in The Broken Middle where she implores intense scrutiny of the thought she recognises as 'postmodern' in its bipolar diremption of law and ethics. Such diremption, she says, leaves the only hope of politics to be 'forced or fantasized' in the middle,[46] emptied of its concept and leaving philosophy to become mere 'social theory'.[47] The hiatus between law and ethics has, in her view, the effect of disabling meaningful thinking about how to organise ourselves in political community. She claims we need, instead, to recognise the actuality of conceptual oppositions, rather than identifying them as radical aporia, and therefore to seek knowledge and understand-ing rather than evading the painful 'risk of coming to know'.[48] Rose's criti-cism of Levinas is that the political/juridical he describes is one orientated by the ungraspable transcendent, whether as the eschatology of peace in Totality and Infinity or as the other that provokes adjudication and the delivery of justice in Otherwise than Being. If the ethical is dirempted, it yields nothing to the immediacy of pre-existent knowledge. Thus, for Rose, it 'can only appear itself as a "disengaged" prescription – holy and without any purchase on "the real world"'.[49]

Rose's polemical critique is somewhat sobering. It may be the case that Levinas's philosophy, by tracing the limits to which we can think and respond to the radical other, does not contain the same normative certi-tude of other political and legal theories. Whether this is fatal to Levinas's relevance for grounded and engaged philosophical thinking might depend on how compelling one finds his analyses of ontology and alterity in the first place. He is, after all, making a series of principally descriptive claims about the human condition. Nevertheless, Levinas does occasionally invite us to interpret a relation between his ethics and broad normative ideas. 'Irrefusable responsibility nonetheless never assumed in complete freedom, is *good*', he writes in the essay 'Humanism and An-archy'.[50] In *Totality and Infinity* he claims that 'goodness' involves 'taking up a position in being such that the Other counts more than myself.'[51] Meanwhile, Levinas spent time reflecting on the meaning of 'evil'.[52] What is the precise meaning of terms like 'good' here? It is predictably characteristic of Levinas to employ a familiar term of language and then immediately make clear that he means it in a sense entirely different to that likely to be most intuitive. The 'good', for Levinas, is not an indicator of a superior moral choice. The good simply refers to the way in which subjectivity is inclined towards the other in a relationship of constitutive responsibility. We desire the good insofar as we are orientated towards the infinite in our ethical responsibility, and therefore find that the otherwise-than-being is 'better than being'.[53] The good, in this sense, is a description of the structure of ethical subjectivity. At the beginning of *Otherwise than Being* Levinas confirms that 'the Good cannot become present or enter into a representation' and, because it 'is not presented to freedom', it can be concluded that 'no one is Good voluntarily'.[54] Anyone searching for a political or legal programme of justifiably 'right' behaviour in this idea of the good is pursuing a particularly stubborn wild goose.

Ultimately Levinas's ethics are descriptive in seeking to explain not what we ought to do, or to whom we owe ethical duties, but instead how we come to be bound to others. On the whole, legal norms tend to hold people accountable for choices. Criminal law, for instance, is built upon the pillars of *actus reus* and *mens rea*, the latter of which attributes culpability for varying degrees of individual voluntariness in people's behaviour (there are some notable exceptions of course, such as offences of strict liability, or the law's forays into objective standards of recklessness).[55] Private law similarly offers remedies against parties who break voluntary agreements (contract), or act against conscience (equity), or perform a whole host of possible deliberate actions that cause harm to others (tort). Levinas's ethics, by contrast, bind us prior to choice and fall outside the scope of the normative dimension of decision-making. They do not provide a cognisable formula for making good choices – only that the other can bind us into a situation in which a choice must be made.

Conscious decisions, whether moral, political or legal, all exhibit a form of ontological violence in their inevitable assimilation of the radical ethical demand.[56]

But could it not be argued that the very imperative to heed the call of the other, irrespective of the content of the other's needs, provides a set of distinct (although rather loose) normative ideas? Whilst ethics might not generate determinate norms, one might claim that the very responsiveness of the ethical condition has the effect of shepherding us towards certain ways of treating others. At the most basic level, could one derive from Levinas's work a normative law of fidelity to alterity, for instance? Does an openness to otherness, which is unconditional and prior to freedom, necessarily lead us to a substantive norm of hospitality, and if so, can this be developed with even greater opacity into laws that promote tolerance, cosmopolitanism, mutual respect? And if so, how far could this be transposed into familiar legal fields, for instance around immigration, human rights, or private law obligations? This question raises an important matrix of issues around Levinas's relevance to legal norms generally. If there is, in this sense, a porosity between the formal nature of the ethical injunction and the substance of normative ideas, it forces us to confront the difficult limit between a theory that explains how we are ethical and one which tells us what such an ethics requires of us. Such questions will be taken up further when examining the application of Levinas's ethics to substantive legal issues in the next chapter.

A subsidiary question that ought to be asked is whether legal norms need a foundation in some form of ethical encounter. In other words, irrespective of precise content, must the authority of law be derived from a prior ethical experience that has gone through the passage of justice? One commentator who has explored this question specifically, Jonathan Crowe, concluded affirmatively that '[t]he obligatory character of law depends upon its ethical content'.[57] The argument begins by holding legal (as well as moral) norms to depend on a certain form of normative weight in gaining their obligatory character. In the light of Levinas's work, Crowe argues, ethics provides the context for the normative language we use in justifying the authority of such norms. Law can neither close itself off from this role of ethics, but nor can it assimilate ethics. Law must, therefore, be constitutively open to what Crowe portrays as an inescapable influence of ethics: 'It follows that ethical meaning permeates the legal context from the outset'.[58] What authorises the legal system as a whole is characterised as a type of a Kelsenian 'basic norm', a fundamental standard from which all other norms derive their validity, and which is itself not dependent on any higher norm. For Crowe, such a basic norm, if it exists, is the very openness of law to the wisdom of ethics. Similarly, Reena Goyal has argued that Levinas allows us to modify traditional positivist justifications of law, Kelsen and Hart included, by shifting from an idea of the objective metaphysical validity of law to a justification grounded in the human encounter.[59] If we accept this, it follows that what makes law binding upon us as individuals is the history of ethical weight that influences it. Upon this view, ethics might not tell us precisely what the content of laws ought to be, but nevertheless the ethical experience is an underlying condition of law coming into being.

A number of further questions arise, however. First, what is the status of legal norms that defy ethical experience? When a law is passed that, to pose a despairingly familiar example, restricts civil liberties and *habeas corpus* under the dubious exigency of combating terrorism, it is surely impossible to claim that such a law bears the weight of Levinasian ethics. As this presumably receives no authority from this basic norm, and notwithstanding how we might find such law to be problematic in political terms, can we then conclude that there is no philosophical obligation to follow this particular law? Secondly, the passage from ethics to law must be revisited. When claiming that 'ethical meaning permeates the legal context', or '[l]egal discourse is particularly vulnerable to infiltration by ethical meaning',[60] one has to be careful not to elide the very indeterminacy of the difficult hiatus between the ethical and the juridical, discussed earlier in this chapter. This is, of course, a persistent issue for Levinasian jurisprudence in general.

This sort of approach situates Levinas in a curious intermediary space between natural law and legal positivism. On the one hand, there is a positivistic concern to be able to identify binding law within a posited institutional framework. On the other hand, if the ultimate norm within such a framework is presented as something akin to 'ethical openness', where ethics is distinctly not capable of being reduced to a legal norm without remainder, then it is impossible to resist the claim that it is essentially a form of natural law theory. The posited system of law as a whole is authorised by a transcendent imperative to be responsive to ethical demands. Does this mean that we can conceive of Levinas himself as a natural law theorist? Such an outlook would not be out of place within a recent revival of interest in natural law ideas in philosophical legal studies recently, typically involving continental philosophy being read as an exposition of a higher, deeper, more originary law.[61] Whilst the constitutive gap between ethics and positive law must be affirmed, it remains at the very least open to suggest that the ethical demand, a fundamental responsibility and hospitality that inheres in the human condition, might serve as a critical plumb line, a natural law that positive law must strive (and always to some extent fail) to do justice to.

Sidestepping the problematic invocation of 'nature' that this entails (to be taken up in Chapters 5 and 6), there remain a few problems with this position, however. First, trying to configure ethics and law in this way does not solve the problem that ethics fails to give a reason as to why we should be ethical. Alphonso Lingis's way of formulating this, writing in the translator's introduction to *Otherwise than Being*, is that '[t]he sense of the law as an imperative is caught up in the obedience itself ... I find myself obedient to the law before it has been pronounced'.[62] If that becomes the case, there is no sense in asking why anyone should bother following this law, or why ethics (as 'natural law') becomes a justifiable measure of the law's legitimacy, because the normative questions of law's content and validity are negated. One can still ask, though, why positive law should seek to be guided by its ethical, 'natural' counterpart. One answer might lie in a muddy idea of authenticity. This position would entail something along the lines of the following: to be ethical is to be true to an immutable, descriptive characteristic of what it means to be human, therefore we should enact positive laws to enable their alignment with this understanding of the human condition. As Levinas said, to try to evade the unconditional responsibility one has for the other is a denial of oneself and one's own uniqueness.[63] Framing the argument in this way is reminiscent of political philosophies that aspire to the idea of human 'flourishing' as an end in itself.[64]

This leads us to a related problematic though, which is that if you need a law to make people act ethically, then this is not really an ethics in Levinas's sense. It should be absolutely clear that no compulsion to act ethically, to undo the self in the complex structure of substitution, can be effectuated by a law decreed by the state. When Levinas, in one of his scattered direct reflections on law, talks of a legal structure in which subjectivity 'enters with the dignity of the citizen into the perfect reciprocity of political laws that are essentially egalitarian',[65] it is apparent that he is not claiming that an ethical sensibility ought to be reflected in the directive force of legal norms. Rather, the rule of law works to provide a social platform in which people can express their ethical disposition to each other. The hope for law is not, therefore, to enforce an ethics, nor to articulate an ethics substantively, but to guard society against the ever-present risk of totality, of a state apparatus that forgets the other, even in apparently benign political environments where a façade of harmony derives from a banal ontological fixity.

Anarchic Ethics

Having offered a slightly cautious reading of the idea that Levinasian ethics can be situated either in the institutions or the very norms of law, this chapter concludes by examining an alternative perspective. This is to suggest that the most apt significance Levinas has for law instead lies outside law's being, operating as the critique of law, or a spirit of rebellion. This involves not merely focusing on the basic configuration of ethics' power to disrupt the ontological certitude of law, but also to account for the risk that Levinas clearly identified in the law's ability to forget the other in a perpetual reproduction of the same.[66]

Posing an anarchic character to Levinas's ethics is an analytical exercise with respect to his philosophy, not his politics. The concept of anarchy, which Levinas uses in a manner that is distinct, or more specifically 'prior', to its political meaning,[67] makes an occasional appearance particularly in his later writings, most notably the essay 'Humanism and An-archy', as well as within the central arguments of *Otherwise than Being*. Levinas uses anarchy to describe the way that subjectivity might evade the twin problems of a brutally materialist anti-humanism on the one hand, and an essentialism of traditional humanism on the other.[68] Describing the subject's assignment of pre-original responsibility as 'anarchic', Levinas traces a 'humanism of the other', in which being human has a sense and a structure to it that prevents it becoming lost in the anonymity of materialism, but is not reduced to the totalising ontology he associates with the predominant Western philosophical tradition.[69] Levinas describes the subject's 'obedience to an order accomplished before that order makes itself heard: anarchy itself'.[70] This is to accord with the demands of responsibility not because it delineates a principle of obligation, or a benevolent moral choice. The anarchic saying that provokes responsibility does not naturally coagulate into any sort of law or legal doctrine. On the contrary, it is the very disturbance of law's ontology. Here, the work of Miguel Abensour must be noted, in its analysis of anarchy's capacity for 'metapolitical' disruption. To the extent that it signals a politics, it is the very disturbance or departure from politics. As such, Levinas circumvents the familiar contradiction of anarchy, that it must cohere into a principle that effaces its own anarchic nature. By deploying anarchy prior to principle, Levinas ensures that it always escapes this tendency.[71]

Anarchy as it appears in Levinas's framework requires us to revisit his ideas of time. It describes the manner in which responsibility precedes and interrogates the freedom of the subject, and therefore undermines its spontaneity and the sense that the subject's beginning takes place within its own sovereign domain. By virtue of this sense of being ethically bound before having any choice in the matter, '[i]t is as though there were here something before the beginning: an *an-archy*'.[72] But whilst anarchy is prior to choice and to the question of freedom, Levinas nevertheless also describes the substitutive relation with the other as 'anarchic liberation',[73] which frees the subject from being rooted to itself. The freedom found here is, of course, not the sovereign freedom of the autonomous self, but a particular modality of freedom in which the subject finds itself constituted by the other.

The precise reason Levinas uses the concept of anarchy to characterise this form of subjectivity, other than his general shift towards a more turbulent evocation of the ethical relation at the time, is explained in *Otherwise than Being*, when he links it to his much better-known ideas on proximity. This he describes as '*anarchically* a relationship with a singularity without the mediation of any principle, any ideality'.[74] Anarchy therefore signals the one-to-one relation that affects and expresses meaning without being framed through a representable ontological structure. It is the resistance to the established said through the irruptive force of saying. Anarchy is therefore rooted in the radicality of the intersubjective, rather than finding its primary meaning in a principled resistance to state authority.

Levinas denies that anarchy presents a picture of chaos against the more orderly realm of the ontological said. This false dichotomy would fail to understand that disorder is a thematisable structure, just as is order.[75] Transcending this distinction, anarchy affects the subject before this pairing becomes sensible. Subjectivity is anarchic at root. It not only resists being's essence, but moreover operates *as* that very resistance. Whilst the work of subjectivity can bring law into being, what remains more fundamental, it can therefore be suggested, is that subjectivity's status as an embodied critique of law. The ethical relation between subject and other, proximity, is constitutive of this anarchic resistance. The point is not to incorporate anarchy into political or legal principle for its own sake, but to recognise it as an unconditional and pre-political disposition that, in the presence of the third and the exigency of the political, allows the subject to be confronted with law's failures and the necessity of its critique. It is therefore important to emphasise the duality of anarchy and justice, as William Simmons puts it, and the continual 'alternating movement' Levinas identifies between the (re)constitution of the said in the domain of law and politics, and its break-up upon the challenge of the other.[76]

Finally, a discussion on anarchy and law cannot ignore the suggestion made by Simon Critchley that Levinas might be capable of supporting an 'anarchic law'. Critchley considers the tension explicated earlier, that the ethical saying cannot be made meaningful in a representable objective sense without the said, but the said, which is the necessary form of law, will always corrupt the saying. Addressing this, Critchley asks whether an anarchic law might be 'a law that has no law at its base and as its basis, where anarchy is understood as the relation of proximity to the neighbour'.[77] Yet such a correspondence of anarchy and law revisits the same issues considered in the previous section, where ethics becomes identified as law's origin or foundation. Critchley himself leaves this idea open and speculative, and it remains unclear precisely how anarchically such a law could operate. It would require a law that is constantly resisting itself, permanently turning itself inside out at its very foundation. What guarantees that this anarchic impetus within law continues? The claim to be developed in the last two chapters and the concluding argument of this book is that to think of the law itself as anarchic, or indeed as a productive site of incorporating an ethics into public life generally, requires a utopianism that distracts us from law's complicity with ideological apparatuses that effectuate the opposite, concretising the same at the expense of the other. Instead, we might understand the anarchic impetus of subjectivity, in the singular experience of the injustice dealt to the other by law, as a perpetual resistance to legal ontology in its ethical torsion.

Notes

1. Levinas, *Is it Righteous to Be?*, p. 56.
2. Levinas, *Totality and Infinity*, p. 279.
3. Ibid., p. 280.
4. Ibid., p. 285.
5. Ibid., p. 300.
6. Levinas, *Otherwise than Being*, p. 157.
7. Ibid.
8. Ibid.
9. Levinas, *Alterity and Transcendence*, p. 143.
10. Levinas, *Entre Nous*, pp. 88–9.
11. Levinas, *Otherwise than Being*, p. 158.
12. Simmons, 'The Third', p. 96.

13. Levinas, *Otherwise than Being*, p. 160.
14. Ibid., p. 45.
15. As Simon Critchley succinctly formulates this, '[i]f ethics without politics is empty, then politics without ethics is blind' (Critchley, *Ethics, Politics, Subjectivity*, p. 283). Howard Caygill articulates this structure in similar terms: 'in order for there to be justice, ethics must be supplemented by ontology and ontology by ethics' (Caygill, *Levinas and the Political*, p. 131).
16. Critchley, *Ethics, Politics, Subjectivity*, p. 275.
17. Wolcher, 'Ethics, Justice, and Suffering in the Thought of Levinas', p. 114.
18. Levinas, *Entre Nous*, p. 89.
19. Levinas, 'Paradox of Morality', p. 175.
20. Levinas, *Alterity and Transcendence*, p. 143; In fairness to Levinas, however, it might be asked how dissimilar this is to Ronald Dworkin's claim that the work of the judge's interpretive role is to weave their judgment into a continuously adapting seamless whole.
21. Levinas, *Totality and Infinity*, p. 300.
22. Levinas, *Otherwise than Being*, p. 165.
23. For an analysis of the various expressions of linear temporality in law, see Ali Khan, 'Temporality of Law'. See also Wistrich, 'The Evolving Temporality of Lawmaking'; French, 'Time in the Law'.
24. Greenhouse, 'Just in Time'. Contrast with an alternative account which claims various non-linear forms of time are observable within legal processes (French, 'Time in the Law').
25. Douzinas, 'Theses on Law, History and Time', p. 24.
26. Levinas, *Otherwise than Being*, p. 37.
27. Ibid.
28. For similar reflections on law and time, see Douzinas, 'Theses on Law, History and Time'; Fish, *Doing What Comes Naturally*.
29. Levinas, *Otherwise than Being*, pp. 38–43.
30. Ibid., p. 38.
31. Ibid., p. 36.
32. It is incidental to the point being made, but in any case, the relevant authority in English law is *R v. Woollin* [1999] AC 82.
33. See, for example, Brooks and Gewirtz, *Law's Stories*.
34. Levinas, *Otherwise than Being*, p. 159.
35. *R v. R* [1991] 1 AC 599, p. 616.
36. Ibid., p. 623.
37. Ibid.

38. Fitzpatrick, *Modernism and the Grounds of Law*, p. 88.
39. For our purposes, and without seeking to (mis)represent Fitzpatrick's position, the origin may be historical, as a real event that brought a legal structure into being, but also may be logical, as a root concept such as good faith or causation.
40. On the nature of the origin in the processes of justice, see Ciaramelli, 'Comparison of Incomparables'.
41. *R v. R*, p. 611.
42. Levinas, *Otherwise than Being*, p. 160.
43. Levinas, *Alterity and Transcendence*, p. 143.
44. Perpich, 'Getting Down to Cases', p. 34. See also Perpich, *The Ethics of Emmanuel Levinas*, chapter 4. On the problem of trying to divine a practical political normativity from Levinas's work, see also Diamantides, 'Levinas and Critical Legal Thought', p. 183; Alford, 'Levinas and the Limits of Political Theory', p. 121.
45. Applying Levinas to questions of policy is made especially complex as the author/subject must avoid the inclination to present and totalise the relation with the other. What is required is the prioritisation of affective experience, in which the subjects cease to see the other as a term within a closed economy of meaning, and allow themselves to be implicated, accused and responsible, in the encounter with the other. Wainer argues that this approach demands the writing and re-writing of this experience, in a project of consciousness-raising, rather than reducing the other to an object of theory within tangible policy recommendations (Wainer, 'Beyond the Wire', p. 5).
46. Rose, *The Broken Middle*, p. xii.
47. Ibid., p. xiii.
48. Ibid.
49. Ibid., p. 263. Elsewhere, Rose speculates on the appeal of an ethics that transcends the rationality and structure of politics, arguing that it is clearly seductive in a world where we so commonly perceive our situation as one of subjugation at the hands of the state. But in 'evading the risks of political community' by turning to an ethics of the absolute other, Rose argues that one detaches oneself from the real business of politics altogether (Rose, *Mourning Becomes the Law*, p. 36).
50. Levinas, 'Humanism and An-archy', p. 53
51. Levinas, *Totality and Infinity*, p. 247.
52. See Levinas's essay 'Transcendence and Evil' in *Of God Who Comes to Mind*.

53. Levinas, *Of God Who Comes to Mind*, p. 69.
54. Levinas, *Otherwise than Being*, p. 11.
55. See *R v. Caldwell* [1982] AC 341 and *R v. G and Another* [2003] UKHL 50.
56. For a discussion of the apparently deterministic nature of such ethics, in contrast to the idea of making free moral choices, see Atterton, 'Levinas's Skeptical Critique of Metaphysics and Anti-humanism'.
57. Crowe, 'Levinasian Ethics and Legal Obligation.' p. 432. See also Crowe, 'Levinasian Ethics and the Concept of Law'.
58. Crowe, 'Levinasian Ethics and Legal Obligation', p. 430.
59. Goyal, 'Serving Justice through Authority.' In a similar vein, see three pieces by William Conklin: 'The Invisible Author of Legal Authority', 'The Trap', and 'The Trace of Legal Idealism in Derrida's Grammatology'.
60. Crowe, 'Levinasian Ethics and Legal Obligation', p. 430.
61. For instance, on Derrida, see de Ville, 'Rethinking the Notion of a "Higher Law"'. And on Heidegger, see Ben-Dor, *Thinking About Law*. For commentary on this trend, see Stone, 'Life Beyond Law'.
62. Lingis, 'Translator's Introduction', in Levinas *Otherwise than Being*, p. xxiii.
63. Levinas, *Otherwise than Being*, p. 122.
64. E.g. the literature on virtue ethics, one prominent example of which is MacIntyre, *Dependent Rational Animals*.
65. Levinas, *Alterity and Transcendence*, p. 143.
66. This is evident in, for example, his reference to the 'universal rules' that judge the subject and the other when the political is bounded by totality (*Totality and Infinity*, p. 300), the tendency of even just legal decisions to slip back into the expression of the anonymous *there is* (*Otherwise than Being*, p. 163), and the way that a society 'without justice' can nevertheless be ordered and 'balanced' by its laws (*Of God Who Comes to Mind*, p. 9).
67. Levinas, *Otherwise than Being*, p. 194.
68. Levinas describes anti-humanism as tending towards the erasure of subjectivity in favour of a 'non-human order, suited to the name that is anonymity itself: matter' (Levinas, 'Humanism and An-archy', p. 48).
69. Levinas, 'Humanism and An-archy'.
70. Ibid., p. 54.
71. Abensour, 'An-archy between Metapolitics and Politics'. See also Critchley, *Infinitely Demanding*; Critchley, 'Anarchic Law'. For fur-

ther discussion of this tension within anarchic or anarchist ideas of law, see Stone, 'Law, Ethics and Levinas's Concept of Anarchy'.

72. Levinas, *God, Death and Time*, p. 172.
73. Levinas, *Otherwise than Being*, p. 124.
74. Ibid., p. 100, original emphasis.
75. Ibid., p. 101.
76. Simmons, 'The Third'. This reference to alternating movement is found in *Otherwise than Being*, p. 165.
77. Critchley, 'Anarchic Law', p. 210.

4

Adjudication, Obligation and Human Rights: Applying Levinas's Ethics

This chapter will instantiate some of the discussion in the last by providing a critical reading of existing literature on how, and to what extent, Levinas can be turned to directly legal questions in a more grounded fashion. There are three principal approaches that this chapter will explore: first, the idea that Levinasian ethics can be embodied within the state apparatus of the judiciary; secondly, that such ethics can inhere in our civil legal relations with other private citizens; and thirdly, we can examine the specific literature, prompted by Levinas's own writings, that suggests ethical responsibilities can be protected by human rights. The chapter will conclude with a brief consideration of some peripheral applications in animal rights, healthcare law and immigration law.

The Ethics of Legal Judgment

As Robert Gibbs has noted, Levinas's passages on 'the third' conceive law as adjudication, such that we do not regard the judge as above the parties to the dispute, as if applying a formula of 'cognitive meta-thought', but as an engaged *part* of the triangular relationship in which the unconditionality of ethics is turned over to the question of justice.[1] To what extent, therefore, can we envisage the judiciary as being ethically implicated in this manner? Such a question does not merely concern how we make legal decisions (as explored in the previous chapter), but also the extent to which the ethical sensibility of such decisions can be institutionalised. Drucilla Cornell was amongst the first to pursue this line of inquiry into justice and legal adjudication. In her 1988 essay, 'Post-Structuralism, the Ethical Relation, and the Law', she argued that although the rationality of law undermines the infinite demand of the ethical, 'it is only the aspiration to the ethical that can give us reason'.[2] In other words, she interprets the antecedence of ethics with respect to ontology, and the simultaneous necessity of ontology (as language, knowledge, law, and so on), as showing the root of just law to be the pre-legal asymmetrical debt to the other. This is a point worth emphasising, as it is at odds with the seductive assumption that the 'beyond' signified in the proximity of the other would somehow expose a nihilistic abandonment of rationality, or that the adjudication of justice requires a discretionary or even arbitrary departure from (legal) reason. In this respect, Cornell's reading of Levinas offers something of a rejoinder to Gillian Rose's sceptical take, considered in the previous chapter. Indeed, Levinas regarded the inclination towards the transcendent other as crucial to reason,[3] as the very condition of novel thinking and a vigilance against the 'bad infinity' of a dispassionate rationality that assumes it has no exterior.[4] In Cornell's subsequent book, *The Philosophy of the Limit*, she elaborated on these themes by situating them more squarely within the domain of the judge. As an ethically exposed subject, the judge is accountable for their decision in a manner that extends beyond a purely formal application of totalised legal rationality. To conflate the position of the judge with such a procedural systemic rationality risks buying into the 'myth of full presence'.[5] In Levinasian language, it is to promote the totality of the same to the subordination of the other. On the contrary, the judicial role is exceptionally suited to embody the capacity for judgment that seeks to do justice to ethical demands.

If such a capacity is expressed more easily in appellate judgment, it is fitting that Cornell concludes that a form of ethics owed to both Derrida and Levinas was at play in the United States Supreme Court decision of *Roe* v. *Wade*.[6] This case famously recognised women's right to have an abortion by virtue of the right to privacy contained in the Fourteenth Amendment of the Constitution. At first glance this decision is vulnerable to an accusation of judicial invention. One could object that the Justices seemed simply to draw out whichever provision of the Constitution could be contorted to lend support for their desired outcome. Such an interpretation was effectively put forward in the dissenting opinions. Whilst an approach of this sort is not necessarily indefensible for a legal realist, it would nevertheless seem to undermine the law's internal coherence. On the contrary though, Cornell claims that the act of judgment here is considerably more complex than retroactively justified creativity, and evinces a type of responsibility that would be wholly absent from a mechanical application of existing precedents. As Levinas has it, time is given by the time of the other, the ungraspable diachrony of that which is beyond the same, and beyond the present. Cornell, drawing a parallel (although not a full equivalence) between Levinas's and Derrida's conceptions of time, argues for an understanding of the link between temporality and justice. She argues that justice must come from the other, and thus from an-other time, such that it can offer the promise of meaningful transformation.[7] Insofar as the responsibility inherent in judgment must aspire to justice, the work of memory in judging, in which precedents and codes are interpreted, cannot be divorced from the responsibility for justice's futurity. For Cornell, 'when the judge remembers the past she does so through the "ought to be" implicit in the not yet of the never has been'.[8] Judging cannot be limited to a continuous linearity of precedent, as justice is always addressed to a future that is other. Moreover, for Cornell this is a justice that is directly and immediately implicated in judges' interpretations of past cases and established sources of law. Cornell therefore expresses not merely a faith in the idea that the judiciary can be affected by the ethical demand, but moreover, that this is a core part of what the responsibility and integrity of judicial office demand.

By requiring the judge to assume accountability for the radical 'not yet', Cornell breaks with the linear conception of time dominant in modernity.[9] Further implications for Levinas's possible resistance to the modern legal tradition have been examined by Costas Douzinas and Ronnie Warrington. They claim that 'the modern conception of justice is no longer that of *dikē*, the social face of the ethics of intersubjectivity; it becomes exclusively *social* justice, an artificial way of organising the social order when its traditional bases have been weakened'.[10] Addressing this question, the authors see something of an equivalence between the ethical position of Antigone, the figure of Greek mythology, and Levinas's ethics. Antigone's ethical gesture takes place when she buries the body of her brother, Polynices, doing so against the official decree that he must suffer the indignity of an unceremonious death for his crimes against the city of Thebes. In Douzinas and Warrington's reading of the legend, *dikē*, a form of justice associated with the moral wisdom of the goddess *Dikē*, is not a code with which Antigone accords in the act of burial. Rather, Antigone creates justice by pursuing the ethical bond that exists between herself and her brother.[11] It is a singular intersubjective act whose justice can never be fully transposed into law. This act, the authors argue, contrasts with the justice of modernity, which depends on formality, symmetry and a preference for an abstract rationality that conveniently obviates the necessity of the face-to-face encounter.[12]

Douzinas and Warrington therefore regard the judiciary as an institution that can renew this face-to-face dimension to justice. The courtroom, in which parties are able to express themselves and tell their stories, revealing the nudity of their alterity, represents an especial site in which the affective encounter can take place. The particular role of the judge incorporates the unique, interpersonal relation, in which Douzinas and Warrington identify the possibility of Levinasian ethics to interrupt the pervasive ontology of law. They describe a 'judge [that] is always involved and implicated, called upon to respond to the ethical relationship when he judges'.[13] The duty of the judge therefore arises out of the presence of the third and the necessary relationship between both the singular ethical relationship with an other and the duty to simultaneously limit and extend responsibility in the form of general principle or rule.

However, Douzinas and Warrington's analysis also provides the resources for an important distinction to be drawn out between the justice of Antigone and the justice of the Levinasian judge. Antigone's justice is devoted to a singular other. It is a justice that arises out of an ethical commitment to a specific person that persists even in its manifest illegality. Hers is an act not of law, but of resistance, an attack on the authority of law by investing one's acts in the radical drive of ethics. Antigone points us to the necessity to not forget the other within the technicality and abstraction of law, but she herself is not the judge, and the judge cannot afford to make the same abyssal sacrifice as her. A Levinasian justice of adjudication, on the other hand, may involve ethical demands being placed upon the judge, but to a crucial extent is a type of procedural justice. It demands, as Levinas said, the weighing and comparing of competing ethical demands, of the priority of others, and the necessity of weaving the ethical call of the other into the ontology of law, as illustrated by Cornell's example of the Supreme Court reasoning. This poses an important tension, between a reading of Levinas which teaches the judge the true meaning of justice in law, or one that instead lures them into effacing law in the role of the rebel, reflecting what Marinos Diamantides refers to as a 'judicial failure to stick to the legislative script'.[14] In the latter sense, the judge does not resemble the earnest, lofty arbiter of the fate of law in the aporetic dilemmas of justice, but a figure of 'foolish excellence', whose ethical sensibility turns judgment into a productively absurd spectacle.[15]

There is further room for some cynicism about the proclivity of the judiciary to grapple with the demands of justice in this manner. First, the alterity of a party to the hearing, its potential to express an irruptive saying, must necessarily be put into conflict with that party's representation by legal counsel – representation both in the sense of advocacy but moreover as translation into the language of law. Indeed, the mere prudence of having a representative has the potential to immediately assimilate signification into the legal said, and recalls Levinas's description of representation itself as 'a determination of the other by the same, without the same being determined by the other'.[16] Secondly, why would we trust the judiciary to effectuate the ethical rupture of law's synchrony? For Cornell, the answer may address a commitment to the very integrity of law and its contended origin in the ethical encounter. But if instead we entertain the claim that, as Diamantides emphasises, adjudication requires the effacement of law in a moment of rebellion, we might ask ourselves how anarchic an institution the judiciary can be expected to be.

Ethics and Private Law

There is perhaps good reason to think that Levinas might be able to tell us something about private law. After all, private law articulates a set of norms that address people's relationships with other people. Whilst it would be a mistake to assume that this is not also true of much of the criminal law, notwithstanding that the legal relationship is between defendant and state, private law nevertheless expresses something that the prohibitive charters of crime do not: obligation. Whereas the last section was concerned with situating the judge as the subject implicated in the demands of ethics and justice, any attempt to delineate a Levinasian foundation to private law obligation is altogether different. Instead of positing a formal mode of adjudication, it must suggest that Levinasian ethics can generate a set of distinct ideas on how we ought to co-exist. The inherent difficulties of this were introduced in the previous chapter, and will be explored via examples here also.

The most extensive analysis linking an applied area of private law to Levinas's ideas (as well as being probably one of the most sustained arguments on Levinasian jurisprudence generally) is Desmond Manderson's project on the tort of negligence.[17] Whilst dedicated to this one doctrinal field of law, it does also provide some general lessons about how we might apply Levinas to thinking about the legal enforcement of interpersonal duties. The modern framework of tort in the English legal system was famously laid down by *Donoghue* v. *Stevenson* [1932] AC 562, the case of nervous shock suffered by a patron of a Paisley café who unwittingly consumed the partially decomposed remains of a snail inhabiting her ginger beer bottle. She successfully sued the drink manufacturer, despite the lack of any direct contractual relationship with them. This was achieved through the House of Lords' formulation of the 'neighbour principle', holding that one has a duty of care over those who can be reasonably foreseen to be affected by one's actions; in other words, those within our proximity.

This, Manderson holds, is precisely one of the reasons why Levinas is helpful in elucidating the normative weight of tort law. It addresses duties that arise without agreement or reciprocity, but rather from the impact of our presence and individual freedom upon others, the way that our actions place us in responsibility for those around us. In particular, tort law gives juridical effect to our proximities to each other. One recalls a poetic line of Levinas's about the unassumed and unintended consequences of our most everyday actions.

> Reaching out my hand to pull a chair toward me, I have folded the arm of my jacket, scratched the floor, and dropped my cigarette ash. In doing what I willed to do, I did a thousand and one things I hadn't willed to do.[18]

Our presence is therefore not one of withdrawn personal freedom, as if one can step back from the world into an isolated domain. We are always embedded in situations where our agency affects others, and for which we are accountable. One can see the appeal of thinking of Levinas as the tort lawyer, as a theorist of obligations that arise not out of voluntary office or contract, but from the simple fact that we are situated such that our actions implicate us in the fate of the other.

Some striking points of common language are shared between tort jurisprudence and Levinas's philosophy that make their comparison especially tempting (for instance 'neighbour', a term Levinas came to use to describe the relation with the other person, not to mention 'proximity'). However, this does lead Manderson into something of a double bind. Having posited the idea of negligence as being derived from a broadly Levinasian structure of obligation, he has then to criticise the many instances in which the juridical and philosophical constructions of proximity manifestly fail to converge fully.[19] Once an obligation between individual persons becomes entrenched in law, it is difficult to see how it retains a strong ethical status in Levinasian terms.[20] If tort law encourages us to be mindful of the consequences of our actions upon others, is this down to ethics or the desire to avoid legal penalties? Again, we revisit the difficulty in conceiving law as something that directs us into adopting an ethical position by compulsion. Or, alternatively, is there an ethical residue in the act of paying damages in instances where the duty of care has been breached? Proximity in law is a legal construction that authorises a court to require an unwilling party to remedy some harm they have caused. Proximity is for Levinas anarchic and prior to any principle.[21]

This is perhaps a facetious point to make, because as Levinas makes absolutely clear, the intelligible entrenchment of duties in legal rules can only occur within the said. If rules aspire to justice, they must follow through the passage from ethics to law, at best carrying with them an ethical trace that fails to fully signify the infinite chasm of responsibility inherent in the proximal relation with the other. But this, in turn, reveals a greater problem with any attempt to elucidate our ethical interrelations in law. It would be fair to say that the most fundamental lesson of Levinas is that ethics arises in, and constitute, subjectivity. But who is the ethical subject, and what role do they play in the development of the principles of negligence? It cannot be the judge, because, as a branch of private law, the judge is describing someone else's ethical responsibility to another private person. But it is the judge, not the respective defendants in private law actions, that delineates the extent of legal responsibility. The 'problem of passage' in this sort of position is doubled. Not only do we face the initial difficulty, present in Levinas's own ideas, of how a legal said can carry the residue of an ethical saying. We also have the problem that the dilemma of the legal decision, the burden of choice, is held by someone who is not subject to, and subjected by, the originary ethical responsibility in the particular relationship in question. The judge must tell the defendant, 'you are responsible, you ought to have acted differently', whilst being external to the scene of ethical provocation.

What we therefore find in negligence is a set of principles that roughly approximate certain Levinasian notions of responsibility in an abstract sense. But it is a challenging process to understand negligence as a set of legal norms derived from the irruptive experience of ethical exposure. If we are to think that negligence gives measured legal expression to traces of the ethical component of the human condition, we might further probe the relation between these two orders. Consider, for instance, the remoteness rule in tort, which holds that damages for negligence are only available where the harm caused was a reasonably foreseeable consequence of the defendant's actions.[22] This requirement of foreseeability imparts a demand of either conscious or what we could call 'constructively conscious' impropriety. Either your liability depends on the fact that you realised your actions would harm the other, or on the fact that you should have realised it (and, by logical extension, had the opportunity to realise it). Yet Levinasian responsibility, within an ethical register, is entirely removed from the idea of foreseeability. It is responsibility before any question of intention, before foresight, before consciousness. Whilst acknowledging Manderson's claim that foreseeability is in fact 'a red herring' in understanding tort,[23] it is still necessary to note that this doctrine is essentially at odds with the idea of Levinasian ethics, in which the subject is constituted in the accusative form, indebted to the other prior to any question of comprehending the causal impact of its actions. Whilst a doctrinal debate over the centrality of the remoteness test should by no means be dismissed, we should at least ask whether this problem instead signifies precisely the antinomy between the orders of ethics and of law. Almost all of the laws of obligation (and indeed crime) construct legal duties at the point where the defendant was conscious, or should have been conscious, of their responsibility or of the impact of their actions upon others. Law tends to hold us responsible for our choices; ethics binds us prior to choice. One would be right to accept the criticism of Levinas's idea of justice and the third for evincing an underdeveloped idea of law,[24] yet there is a risk in identifying a correspondence between ethical responsibility and legal duty, which is that we cover over the fundamental gap between the two orders, in which the anarchic dimension of the ethical saying has the potential to trouble and critique the settled law.

Moving on, given that various themes of possession, dwelling and hospitality run through areas of Levinas's work, it is also useful to test whether he can be applied to questions about property law. In the English private law tradition, it is normal to distinguish obligations from property, as the latter has had a very hard time articulating any sort of duty-driven normative basis. Legal property relations are typically at root property rights, and any correlative duties are merely derivative.[25] Whilst historically, English land law has been built on the idea of relativity of title (one's right to property is measured relative to others' claims over the same asset), the sweeping 1925 reforms and subsequent changes have shifted the balance to a more absolutist model, in which title and rights of use are determined by their registration status, and are less likely to arise through possession.[26]

At a theoretical level, this represents a greater solidification of an ownership-based understanding of property. Both culturally and philosophically, having property has become regarded as a fundamental articulation of what it means to be a person.[27] This correspondence of ontology and property can be traced to the most familiar philosophical justifications of property rights: Locke's linkage of self-ownership and labour;[28] Kant's idea of property as an expression of freedom;[29] Hegel's dialectical constitution of the subject in relation to the exterior world of

objects.[30] Yet the construction of property via a model of ownership prioritises the individual as a rights-holder and market actor such that we lose
a sense of the (inter)personal or affective role of property in determining
the subject,[31] or of the role of property in developing community in a way
that is not subordinated to an aggregation of autonomous individuals.[32] If
a Levinasian perspective on property would, on the contrary, articulate a
basis for property *obligations*, specifically obligations to the other, then it
might address such an ethical vacuity in existing doctrinal expressions of
property, both in theory and practice.

Levinas's closest reflections on property can be found in the passages
of *Totality and Infinity* where he introduces the idea of the dwelling. As
explained in Chapter 2, the dwelling serves as a metaphor for the hypostasis of subjectivity, the subject drawing in on itself in a process of ontological recollection, providing a frame in which the world around it takes on
meaning. Whilst his analysis of the dwelling indulges in spiralling depths
of allegory it is valuable for its consideration of one of the core aspects of
our intuitive senses of subjecthood, which is self-possession. The dwelling
is what gives substance to the subject's idea of itself. Yet it is also what
allows our sense of propriety to be subjected to an ethical challenge.

The recollective function of the dwelling has a synchronic temporal
effect, giving a presence and continuity to the possessions it houses, which
also necessarily belie a relationship with the diachronic other.[33] The possession of property therefore determines an object as part of me and my
world, but its exclusionary effect simultaneously commits an ontological
reduction of alterity. This assimilative violence does not simply reflect
the fact that private possession is by its nature bounded and therefore
puts distance between the self and the other, but also that possession
is a means of sublating otherness itself. How do we relate to the other
through this analytic of property? Answering this entails returning to one
of the crucial structures of Levinas's thinking on subjectivity, which is
the way in which the ontological said reduces the other to the same but
is nevertheless the structure in which responsibility takes on intelligible
meaning. 'Only a subject that eats can be for-the-other, or can signify'.[34]
It is crucial for Levinas that the subject is able to represent itself and its
possessions to itself, just as it is in the self-ownership described by Locke,
and the dialectic of property found in Hegel. But for Levinas, to represent one's possessions to oneself means there must be a non-coincidence
between the two, and it is precisely this separation that allows the subject
to find its possession being challenged by the other.[35] To maintain an
absolute dominium over one's possessions in this scene is to continue to

maintain one's grasp on the world in a way that denies them to the other, and as a result negates the other's very alterity. Therefore, it would be a mistake to think that Levinas is merely counselling us towards some bland prescription of charity or distributive justice, in which private property is merely reallocated between beings. The other is what calls all of this into question. Whilst Levinas mirrors the broadly Lockean linkage of work and possession, arguing that labouring upon the world is a fundamentally ontological act in the way it allows us to grasp things and let them manifest in being,[36] this relation is inverted by the immediate ethical challenge posed to the propriety of possession itself.

Levinas extends the metaphor of the dwelling by describing ethical responsiveness as an injunction to welcome the other into the home. What is more, the subject that takes stock of itself in the dwelling does not do so as an absolute proprietor, but as someone taking refuge in a place that must first offer welcome (again, Levinas tells us it is the feminine other that offers this initial welcome).[37] To fully understand this, we must bear in mind that for Levinas it is ethics, not ontology, that is 'first philosophy'. The hypostatic gathering-in of dwelling, the finding of a home in which one can understand oneself, is not primordial and does not precede the anonymous experience of the *there is*. Recalling the structure of *Existence and Existents* and *Time and the Other*, Levinas returns to the idea that the hypostatising of subjectivity collects oneself into a being that is possessed (by the welcome of the dwelling) and can possess, but at the same time produces the very conditions of interiority and separation in which it finds that the beyond is what truly opens time and freedom.

The idea of dwelling is a typical point of both convergence and resistance in Levinas's work to the legacy of Heidegger, whose later writing famously meditated on the importance of home.[38] Heidegger saw dwelling as a means of a more authentic and rooted means of being in the world, pitted against the increasingly frequent phenomenon of a kind of existential homelessness in modern living. Levinas, by contrast, understands dwelling as a site of refuge that is not only already occupied, but is also instantly contested by the transcendent other as soon as it provides a frame for the subject to situate itself in and possess.[39] It might be of little surprise, then, that Derrida went on to hail *Totality and Infinity* as a whole as being 'an immense treatise *of hospitality*'.[40] This hospitable relation between the self and the other that is subsequently welcomed is a form of teaching. The closed economy of meaning presupposed by the sovereign proprietor is opened up onto transcendence by the other, such that language and representation are not left to be determined by the mastery of the self.[41] Distance is put between the I and its possessions, such that the ontological grasp on those possessions is freed by the other. The products of the subject's work are not 'inalienable possessions';[42] they have an independent existence in an economy of meaning that allows them to signal to the other, and to have significance beyond the interiority of assimilating alterity into the same.

But can any of this tell us something useful about property as it manifests in positive law? Of course, we have to be careful in understanding Levinas's habit, especially around the period of *Totality and Infinity*, of writing in extended, almost tortuous, metaphor. Whereas Locke might talk of the individual's right to own the literal products of their labour, Levinas is talking of dwelling and possession as a modality of ontology and subjectivity. But what must be remembered is that orthodox property theory operates not simply as a series of justifications for property relations being conceived as private property rights, but as a way of understanding ourselves. What grants Locke's theory coherence is a notion of the split and self-possessing subject, constituted as both owner and owned. Therefore, the property one has in one's person can be extended to the products of one's labour. By providing a radically opposed understanding of how subjectivity is formed with respect to possession and others, Levinas could therefore be understood as providing a philosophical platform for alternative property relations, which contest the hegemony of property as the direct expression of personal sovereignty.

There are two key components to this trajectory of thinking, both self-consciously abstract. First, our property is never truly, inalienably ours. Even the dwelling into which we are welcomed, which allows a proprietary framing of the world, is a site to which we arrive as 'refugees'. Property allows us to make sense of ourselves and the world around us, but this conception would staunchly resist the idea that strong and, moreover, exclusive rights of ownership flow forth naturally. Property is constituted interpersonally, and not as an expression of our isolation from each other. In this manner, Levinas would provide opposition not only to orthodox property ideas around ownership, but also to a stream of alternative property theory such as Margaret Radin's. Her work critiques the market-oriented hegemony of property as fungible, exchangeable assets in favour of recognising a form of inalienable personal property.[43] Radin's argument accepts and builds upon the premise of the proprietary subject – the subject being constituted by possession of itself and its property – but by resisting the alienating effect of the market in this way, she necessarily reinforces the sovereign possessory domain of the owner.

Secondly, Levinas counsels us with a clear ethic of expropriation and a deep justification of the irreducibility and primacy of property obligations before property rights.[44] He provides us with potential resources for understanding the violence wrought on others by our possessory grasp on the world, as well as enabling critique of the philosophical justification of private property that assumes the world of objects exists to serve the subject's dominium as proprietor.[45] He challenges us to reimagine property as a source of responsibility and as a modality through which we are placed in inextricable relation with others around us.

Ethics and Human Rights

Despite the brevity of Levinas's direct writings on law, curiously enough he had a fair amount to say on the subject of human rights. Whilst sceptical of any humanism that would be centred on the autonomy of the egotic legal actor, he nevertheless sustained a faith in rights' promise of fulfilling human dignity. It has even been suggested by Roger Burggraeve that human rights are the very 'source of all social, economic, juridical and political order' in his work.[46] Levinas's outlook in this respect is expressed in a number of short, and frankly very similar, articles from the 1980s.[47] The opening premise of one of the pieces, 'The Prohibition of Representation and "The Rights of Man"', gives a good impression as to his general position. It opens with a discussion of the Jewish forbiddance of idolatry, for instance in the artistic representation of God, which works to resist the Western prioritisation of presence in consciousness. The point Levinas takes from this with respect to rights is the way Judaism places spiritual priority on transcendence rather than graspable presence. Such thinking can inform rights discourse by suggesting that a more meaningful human rights is therefore reached if the right of 'man' is first understood as the 'right of the other man'.[48] In other words, 'man' as the present and graspable subject of rights is decentred in favour of measures that seek to protect the transcendent other. This, of course, is a radical reformulation of rights, which would no longer be rooted as positive entitlements of legal entities, but which are expressed in the undischargeable responsibility felt for alterity. Predictably, the full implications for the protection of such rights in positive law are not set out.

By this time, Levinas had already developed what he called a 'humanism of the other', which, as we have already seen, seeks to uphold the human subject whilst rejecting its traditional sovereign and autonomous characteristics, instead inverting it as constitutively indebted to the other. At fault in rights discourse, he tells us, is the prioritisation of the individual as their holder or subject. Since the Enlightenment, this model has encouraged the legitimisation of rights on the basis not of a social bond, but of each person's individual freedom. The 'rights of man' are the rights to free will, and thus, inevitably, rights to freedoms whose enforcement operates against the freedoms of others. If rights achieve peace it is by virtue of an unstable set of compromises between competing rights-holders, whose freedoms are perpetually limited with respect to each other.[49] The specific political danger of this is twofold. First, it may lead not to a new state of freedom, but to the curtailment of people's liberty. Technological advancement, rather than emancipating the human from her material needs and providing the social grounds for a greater respect for people's dignity, may instead lead to the intensified subjugation of people in the governmental practices of a highly industrialised and weaponised society.[50] The second and more fundamental criticism Levinas levels is against the characterisation of the autonomous human subject from which modern rights discourses have been extrapolated. Justice should not be reduced to a schema of pure logical calculation between the interests of independent entities within a bounded economy of meaning.[51] By seeking to protect the marginalised by entering them into the arena of law, imbuing them with legal presence, human rights law no doubt has led to innumerable victories for victims of state oppression that should not be dismissed. But Levinas helps us understand its severe limitation. Human rights law ontologises people as juridical, entitled entities but is unable to comprehend that which is other to that very ontology. The necessarily excluded suffer a double violation: first from their initial situation of marginalisation, and secondly by their failure to be understood or even recognised within human rights law, leaving them as the ultimate other, otherwise-than-human.[52]

Whilst rights may have become reified as representations of the interests of the individual, Levinas wishes to revisit their original signification, the way in which they articulate a more fundamental dignity to humankind whose *a priori* character is 'prior to ... all jurisprudence.'[53] This is a humanity found in the transcendence and proximity of the other, while the experience of individuality, sovereignty and autonomy takes on only secondary importance. Rethinking rights in this manner demands critique of some of their most familiar characteristics. Consider freedom itself, for example. The freedom that is to be located in rights should not be the empty and impotent freedom of the individual, but the freedom of escaping one's enchainment to oneself, and finding oneself in the other. As such, antecedent to the manifestation of rights in terms of concrete and opposing entitlements, rights may be founded on a basic fraternal ethical responsibility.[54] Such rights must express the *'for-the-other* of the social'.[55]

In this way, rights would reveal themselves to be a means to give effect to the responsible relation with the other, and in doing so introduce the ethical provocation of transcendence into political structures. The necessarily 'extra-territorial' character of asserting such rights 'defines the liberal state and describes the modality according to which the conjunction of politics and ethics is intrinsically possible'.[56] The project of human rights cannot be exhausted by the work of law and politics, but Levinas regards a liberal state as the necessary ground upon which the rights of the other can be expressed. Elsewhere, he is even bolder. Human rights articulate 'a non-state institution inside the State – an appeal to humanity which the state has not accomplished yet'.[57] There is, therefore, a curious relationship between the radical dimension to rights and the institutional framework necessary for them to become meaningful. Levinas is describing rights as operating through the freedoms granted by the liberal state, even though rights may be 'extra-territorial' in nature and do not need to be conferred by a state in order to be asserted.[58] Levinas is never fully clear on the technical operation of the rights of the other, but it appears one can discern a couple of important characteristics. First, the original 'right of the other' effectively describes the primacy of the other in his conception of human dignity, and the way in which one's identity and freedom is entwined with the fate of the other. Secondly, the assertion of concrete rights may give a form of political expression to the other's freedoms – not necessarily in the form of law, but certainly including law, operating on the plane of the social in the presence of the third. The question of what this entails in practice is, characteristically, left open.

One should not be uncritical of Levinas's work in this area, however. In alluding to a link between the basic sociality of ethics and the practical significance of rights, did Levinas betray the very radicalism of his philosophical position by ontologising the other as a concrete category of vulnerable peoples? Or to put the question the other way around, does Levinas need to thematise the other in this way in order for his theory to have meaningful purchase in the humanitarian uses of law? The latter problem has been put forward recently by William Simmons, who has sought to interrogate Levinas on how successfully he can formulate a rights-based protection of the 'marginalized other'.[59] He claims that in order for Levinas to offer practically useful ideas on how we think about human rights, he and his commentators must abandon the very radicality of his formal understanding of alterity.[60] But if Levinas's other is other to ontology, it is a philosophical other, and cannot translate into the 'other as refugee', or the 'other as the impoverished', or any similar concretisation that would allow the rights of the other to become meaningful in a practical, engaged fashion. Notwithstanding Levinas's references to the realisable 'conjunction' of ethics and politics in the liberal state,[61] such constructions of otherness can only operate upon the terrain of the political, not the ethical. This is an essential implication of Levinas's work, and it is important not to dilute it by characterising alterity with particular, tangible forms of identity, however marginalised.

Holding faith with Levinas, Scott Davidson addresses this issue by claiming that the rights of the other might operate such that 'the other has the unqualified or unconditional right to be heard and to make claims for a specific type of treatment', and also that such rights are upheld via a commitment to our responsibility to the vulnerable, including those whose voices cannot be heard.[62] Such a commitment must also, necessarily, mean that we do not prefigure what is meant by the vulnerable in advance. This means we would abandon the idea of rights as an exclusively juridical, possessive set of entitlements in favour of the much more expansive idea of seeking to guarantee a basic political dignity to those who affect us in encounters of ethical provocation, and who call us to responsibility. A similar interpretation of this predicament is adopted in Costas Douzinas's *The End of Human Rights*. By understanding, with Levinas, that responsibility for the other underwrites both the identity and freedom of the subject, Douzinas affirms a Levinasian 'human rights of the other', in which '[t]he community of human rights is also a community of hostages to the other'.[63] Human rights, instead of signalling the guarantees of individual, autonomous freedom, describe a much more amorphous social commitment to doing justice. For Douzinas, the difficulty of turning such a language of rights into a set of determinate norms is not a problem. For him, human rights articulate a radical natural law that operates not as rule, but as a normative base and aspiration for assessing and critiquing positive law. Rights in this sense therefore give us a vocabulary of political transformation, not a distribution of individual privileges. What they offer is 'the promise of the "not yet", of the indeterminacy of existential self-creation against the fear of uncertainty and the inauthentic certainties of the present'.[64] Such readings are compelling in the way that they seek to retain the radical implications of Levinas's critique of totality. Moreover, they prompt us to question the extent to which rights must be contained within their familiar juridical format. The more faithful we are to Levinas's conception of the other, the less recognisable we find the rights of the other to be.

Miscellaneous Others

Finally, we can consider the appeal of Levinas for conceiving the relation between law and various other instances of alterity. What the following three examples tend to have in common is the way they do not fit neatly within the symmetrist structure of conventional liberal jurisprudence which depicts the political as an aggregate of rational, participatory individuals. Such an outlook reflects a broadly Kantian idea of the universalisation of mutually agreeable principles, or their more contemporary statement in the works of someone such as Rawls. As a framing mechanism for introducing the utility of Levinas in providing an alternative to this mode of thinking, it is helpful to briefly make note of Martha Nussbaum's *Frontiers of Justice*. This text makes the persuasive claim that such symmetrist approaches to political philosophy create a blind spot whereby certain actors are discounted by virtue of their inability to participate or achieve reciprocal recognition in the construction of the principles of justice. Without any engagement with Levinas herself, Nussbaum explores the position of the mentally incapacitated, non-human animals and foreign nationals (invoking the question of global justice). All of these categories reveal certain lacunae of modern political philosophy in failing to account for those who we could broadly describe as voiceless – or at least voiceless within the political context in which their recognition is at stake – and whose suffering therefore expresses a particular asymmetry. It is perhaps little coincidence, therefore, that Levinas has been applied to address the question of ethics and justice in each of these areas.

First then, we can start by considering a Levinasian approach to the law's treatment of those disenfranchised by their medical condition. Despite their apparently unlikely homology, the relevance of Levinas and medical ethics has received notable attention in recent years,[65] no doubt in part due to the analyses of the other's suffering in his work.[66] For Levinas, suffering evokes a particular characteristic of the encounter with the other. The other's suffering escapes a rationality that would allow it to be grasped by the observer. On the contrary, suffering is senseless and useless; it signifies such that its call to responsibility is issued outside of a comprehensible order of meaning. Yet the senselessness of suffering is precisely what makes difficult its transposition into the rationality of law. As William Conklin has argued in his reading of Levinas, suffering is neutralised by law insofar as law relies upon a 'representation of suffering [that] sanitizes the pain and redirects it as a meant object of professional knowers'.[67] There is, then, a fundamental antinomy that holds that the cost of the law responding to suffering is the erasure of the very condition of that suffering. It is not merely that the law is imperfect at comprehending suffering, but that its incomprehensibility is essential to suffering itself.

A systematic analysis of a Levinasian approach to medical law is offered by Marinos Diamantides. For Diamantides, the crucial ethical question here is of the legal limits of medical intervention in cases where the autonomy of the patient fails to accord with an idealist conception of human subjectivity. For example, in cases where the patient is unable to give proper consent to medical intervention. Patients in a 'persistent vegetative state', facing the decision of whether to be continued on life support or be allowed to die, represent an exemplar of this problematic, and form a central concern in Diamantides' analysis. Such patients exist in the liminal space between being alive and being dead, necessitating law's treatment of them as subjects of law, yet lacking any of the faculties that would give that construction of subjectivity content. By failing to accord with the essence of being expressed by law, Diamantides explains, the patient signifies as otherwise-than-being but still calls upon the law for some form of recognition.[68] For Levinas, both the death and the suffering of another operate as categories of the non-phenomenality of the other's alterity. They are perceived through the passivity of the subject that precedes and escapes the ontological construction of legal meaning in the said and provokes one's unique and irreplaceable responsibility.

What is essential in the position of Diamantides is his measured cynicism about the ability of law to respond to what are exceptional ethical demands. His analysis of the House of Lords' treatment of vegetative patients reveals the manner in which their judgment elided the full radicality of the ethical demand being placed before them, instead choosing to construct the patient as if living, as if an abstract legal subject.[69] The judge in a scene such as this, Diamantidies writes, is 'an autonomous agent of law, an incorrigible calculator of harm and benefit, rights and interests'.[70] Medical law therefore not only represents an especial site of ethical provocation within legal frameworks, but also represents most starkly the realities of law's limitations in responding to the Levinasian injunction, and moreover the inadequacy of a Levinasian jurisprudence being reduced to some general imperative to adopt mere superficially ethical processes of adjudication. Being affected by the suffering of the other person is one of the most Levinasian of experiences, issued from an indeclinable sense of singular responsibility that constitutes us as subjects. It is an experience that struggles to find meaningful expression in the realm of policy, rule, and the rationality of medico-legal knowledge.

Moving to our second issue, it is easy to see, at first, why Levinas's work might not easily translate into literature on the legal protections of animals, for the simple reason that his relation between same and other is conceived as a specifically human relation.[71] We have already explored Levinas's committed yet qualified humanist stance, and the inescapable human dimension to many of his concepts: fraternity, and the significance of the human body to many of his analyses, for instance. Whilst the latter examples might be argued to have a primarily figurative quality, what is more significant is the role of language, the way in which the relation with the other plays out between the saying and the said, and in particular the necessity of a constituted said and representable language to attempt to express the trace of a saying within the social.[72] The crucial and difficult question for any Levinasian animal rights theorist is, therefore, what becomes of language between human and animal. But it is also for similar reasons that Levinas's work has an intuitive appeal in this area; that is, devising some form of ethical relationship based not upon a shared logos but on an asymmetrical and non-reciprocal duty. By conceiving animal rights as merely derivative of our ethical duties, Levinas might help us to circumvent the difficulty in framing the animal as a traditional rights-bearing subject. Such an alternative approach also recognises that the animal's needs cannot be understood within an intelligible linguistic register, instead signifying a radical alterity.

Levinas himself has offered a couple of very brief and, frankly, inconclusive reflections on animality. The first and perhaps most tantalising came in an interview, published under the title 'The Paradox of Morality', during which he was pressed specifically on the ethical status of the animal's face. His response was frustratingly equivocal ('I don't know if a snake has a face'; yet, 'there is something in our attraction to an animal'),[73] and hard to reconcile with his explicit claims elsewhere that the other is a *human* other.[74] It is possible that his lack of a categorical answer is precisely the point – Matthew Calarco draws attention to the way that agnosticism on the question of the other's species leaves the term constitutively open and therefore infinitised.[75] Nevertheless, such an interpretation requires us to say more on the subject than Levinas did himself. A slightly more sustained although still enigmatic reflection is found in Levinas's short and personally reflective piece 'The Name of a Dog, or Natural Rights', in which he speaks of his experience at Fallingbostel labour camp during the war.[76] The cruel and dehumanising acts of the guards are counterposed against the experience of meeting a stray dog, which befriended the group of prisoners and took on the name Bobby. Unlike the guards, he wrote, Bobby was able to recognise that Levinas and his peers were human. Yet Levinas equivocated on the ethical signification of Bobby, instead concluding that whilst he should be remembered as the 'last Kantian in Nazi Germany', he lacked the faculties for moral reasoning.[77]

Whilst Levinas himself had quite explicitly failed to give the question of animals developed thought, it has been argued that he nevertheless provides the resources for fleshing out a model of ethics across species boundaries. As Jonathan Crowe's reflection on this question attests,[78] this is best achieved by focusing on the thematics of *Totality and Infinity*, especially the significance Levinas attributes to the face and, again, to suffering. Naturally, such emphasis has the inevitable effect of deprioritising his later turn to more focused analyses of language and time in *Otherwise than Being*. Crowe rightly points out that one cannot assume a direct equivalence between the ethical demands placed on us by humans and non-humans in Levinas's work, but nevertheless there is something about the non-human animal that is able to raise an analogous ethical provocation. We are all capable of apprehending the affective power of the suffering of a non-human animal. Why would this have any less of an accusative impact upon our freedom than the human-human encounter? If we accept the ethical status of the animal in this way, we presumably lack any significant philosophical obstacle in according an equivalent consideration in the processes of legal justice and rights that a Levinasian jurisprudence demands for humans. There are at least a couple of challenges that need to be surmounted with this sort of position, though. First, if we circumvent the problem of language by reverting to the frameworks of *Totality and Infinity*, the argument inevitably becomes structured around the phenomenology of animal suffering – the perception of an animal which makes a demand of us via its suffering, over which we feel asymmetrical responsibility. Again, we have to acknowledge the problem that this emphasis on the eidetic experience might fail to truly overcome the problem of ontological totality. In other words, by presenting the ethical demand of the animal in terms of what is perceived by the subject, one never fully articulates the radical alterity of the animal other. Whilst this is a well-known general criticism of aspects of Levinas's work, the second problem is more specific to the question of animals, which is to ask how far our ethical inclination towards non-humans extends. By necessarily focusing on the ethical significance of anthropocentric ideas such as the face and suffering, both things that we recognise as similar to us or potentially experienced by us, it is possible that we come to a limit on the type of animal that can prompt an ethical demand. Can we be provoked by the suffering of a lobster, a fish, an insect, and so on? Crowe acknowledges this point by citing a passage from the aforementioned interview, in which Levinas stated that '[i]t is because we, as humans, know what suffering is that we can have this obligation [to prevent animals' suffering]'.[79] But as humans, whilst we can empathise with cats and dogs and other animals that socialise well with us, we cannot easily imagine what it would be like to be a haddock, or a wasp, or a stick insect. It appears, therefore, that a categorical limitation of a Levinasian approach to animal rights is its possible inability to be ethically accountable for what is truly other-than-human. Instead, an account of animal rights finds a basis in Levinas only to the extent that an ethical disposition towards animals manifests in a mode derivative of our inter-human responsibilities.[80] Leaving aside the implicit normative limitations, this is not necessarily a criticism of the descriptive coherence of Levinas's work. On the contrary, it might go some way to explaining why animal rights movements succeed in mobilising the most support for issues around mammals with which we can mostly easily empathise.

Finally, we can briefly think about how Levinas has been applied to questions of the non-citizen, and specifically the refugee. This brings us back to some of the earliest writings on Levinas and law on the subject of asylum applications,[81] but also a handful of more recent writings that have similarly seen Levinas as an appropriate antidote to the impersonal and often cruelly bureaucratic detention of migrants in the UK, Australia and other developed countries.[82] The basic Levinasian argument in favour of a more ethically reflexive asylum system probably needs relatively little explanation at this stage. A subject-position embodied by the state structure of wealthy Western nations is, we are told, capable of being called to account by the unique ethical demand of the refugee. What Levinas helps us with in particular is providing a justification for an alternative policy that is rooted in the basic, human acts of compassion and hospitality which do not seek to totalise or assimilate the other's suffering. A state might not have particular obligations to such parties as if they were their own citizens, but the source of the ethical compulsion does not arise from the claimant as an enfranchised rights-bearing citizen, but precisely as the opposite, as that which is other. In this vein, Douzinas and Warrington chart the failures of UK asylum law in its attempt to rationalise and objectify the fear and suffering of the applicant, which, as Levinas tells

us, always to an important extent resists assimilation into an ontological schema. The ethical failure of asylum law is secured at the moment
the claimant is required to justify their experience in 'an interpretable,
understandable reality that like all reality is potentially shareable by judge
and victim'.[83] Further, as Joseph Pugliese posits, the consequence of a
failed asylum application and subsequent internment is that one can lose
language altogether.[84] No matter how desperate or anguished one's voice
is expressed, its translation into the language of the state turns it into
silence.

What the applications of Levinas share here is a use of his philosophy
to provide an ethical solution to the problem of a posited unethical,
ontologically violent, legal framework. However, there are some reasons
to be cautious with regard to this approach. First, we should recall the
tension, mentioned in the context of Simmons's work earlier, between
the severity of Levinas's philosophical depiction of the other and the
thematic reduction of otherness to an instrumental political concept.
To the extent that an application of Levinas's ethics leads us to think
of the other specifically as the refugee (or the patient, or the animal, for
that matter), we are led away from the very innovation of his theory.
Secondly, consider Derrida's treatment of hospitality, which traces its
etymological significance in the term *hostis*, the stranger that can be
treated as guest or as enemy.[85] There is an initial trace of hostility in
hospitality, in which the guest is welcomed, but in such a way that
acknowledges the proprietary domain of the host. But there is also a
reversal of terms, in that the host becomes bound by the responsibility it
holds over the guest. In a distinctly Levinasian mode of substitution, the
host becomes hostage. (Derrida's analysis links the treatment of hospitality found in *Totality and Infinity* with the more developed conception of
ethical subjectivity drawn in *Otherwise than Being*'s chapter on substitution.) What this points us towards is the important notion that hospitality is much more than an imperative. It is something that permeates the
traumatic structure of subjectivity that operates in the sustained tension
between autonomy and heteronomy, between appropriation and expiation, same and other. Moreover, the welcoming character of hospitality
presumes an autonomous (and in this instance, legally sovereign) entity
that is capable of the welcome. The condition of hospitality, and its
inherent trace of hostility, is that it can be offered only by an entity that
is simultaneously capable of its denial. The condition of offering one's
home is first having a home that is not possessed by others. The gesture of
the welcome assumes propriety over the site in which one is welcomed.

Therefore, every act of constituting a hospitable site is in part an exclusionary act. What does this mean for our insights on asylum law? Levinas cannot merely issue an injunction for asylum law to be more generous, more accepting. First, such a political imperative to be hospitable cannot be guaranteed by his ethics – once again we revisit the problem of passage from ethics to law.[86] But furthermore, by explicating the tense dynamic between an ethics of hospitality and the jurisdictional structure that is capable of its offering, between the unconditional and the conditional form of hospitality, Levinas shows us that if hospitality is to be embodied within law it also demands the undoing of law. Meanwhile, every gesture of hospitality simultaneously reifies the violent power of the border. For law to become the meaningful locus of hospitality it must become charged with the anarchic spirit of its own de-constitution.

Conclusions

A central objective of this chapter has been to provide an overview of the types of legal questions Levinas has been, or might be, mobilised to address. It aims to attest to the enduring appeal of Levinas for legal theorists, to the feeling that a philosopher who provided such a brief, tantalising and yet underdeveloped thinking of law might nevertheless have tapped into something crucial and, moreover, missing from dominant jurisprudential apparatuses. A distinction emerges when the various uses of Levinas are laid out side by side, between those who see the state institutions of law as having an ethical potential, such as in the ethical subjectivity of the judge, and those that see law as a framework of norms that attempt, albeit highly imperfectly, some form of resemblance to the ethical responsibility felt in our relations with each other. Levinas has therefore been read as someone who can say something about both how law works and what law says. By way of a brief closing comment, the chapter has hopefully demonstrated the relevance and utility of Levinasian ethics for thinking about law, but at the same time highlighted some of the severe challenges. The chapter has deliberately not sought to resolve the fundamental strain between the ethical and the juridical that comes to the surface when Levinas's work is instantiated in legal problems. In each example we see the challenge of investing an idea of such radical ethics into law itself (whether into its adjudicatory institutions or into its normative content), in that the law must somehow continually efface itself. The judge must become the anarchic fool. Rules of tort law must seek to articulate the infinitude of ethical responsibility. Property law must become improper. Border laws must deconstitute the borders. The 'rights of man' must become the rights of the other. What the examples evince is an irreducible tension between ethics and law, in which the more one concretises a juridical duty to the other, making it into a more practicable legal measure, the more one erases the radical nature of the other's alterity, and the less one feels the echoes of the original ethical provocation to which the law seeks to do justice. To an extent, this can be understood as a mere reflection of what Levinas has always counselled, that the difference between the saying and the said is so profound as to escape comprehension, and yet ethics needs ontology to find its voice, however distorted. Yet it could also signal a more sombre possibility, and the very real limits of what it means to attempt normative Levinasian jurisprudence. We cannot, deliberately and consciously, turn ethics into law. One cannot philosophise this passage. As soon as we think as lawyers (or at all), we have already left the ethical, affective sphere. We are always too late. We are left to hope that the law we have already, the law that we constitute and that constitutes us, bears a trace of an other that we can never fully see or know.

Notes

1. Gibbs, 'Law and Ethics', p. 92.
2. Cornell, 'Post-Structuralism, the Ethical Relation, and the Law', p. 1626.
3. Levinas, *Totality and Infinity*, p. 219; Levinas, *Otherwise than Being*, p. 167.
4. Levinas, *Of God Who Comes to Mind*, p. 8.
5. Cornell, *The Philosophy of the Limit*, p. 149.
6. 410 U.S. 113 (1973).
7. Cornell, *The Philosophy of the Limit*, p. 137.
8. Ibid., pp. 152–3. Interestingly, Cornell aligns this understanding of the judge's role with a demand for integrity in judging, comparable to the Dworkinian sense. Yet surely, as argued in Chapter 1, a key difference in Dworkin's work is the way his theory insists on repeating the myth of full presence, whereby the right answer is always available, always already there, even where in hard cases it does not manifest obviously in precedent.
9. Greenhouse, 'Just in Time'; more generally, Jameson, *The Seeds of Time*.
10. Douzinas and Warrington, *Justice Miscarried*, p. 167.
11. Ibid., p. 80.
12. Note here the most famous exposition of justice in twentieth-century

Anglo-American political philosophy, John Rawls's A *Theory of Justice*, in which the principles of justice are imagined in the absence of people's real, situated intersubjective experiences.

13. Douzinas and Warrington, *Justice Miscarried*, p. 184.
14. Diamantides, 'Levinas and Critical Legal Thought', p. 198.
15. Ibid.
16. Levinas, *Totality and Infinity*, p. 170.
17. Manderson, *Proximity*; Manderson, 'Emmanuel Levinas and the Philosophy of Negligence'; Manderson, 'Here I Am.'
18. Levinas, *Entre Nous*, p. 3.
19. 'The well-rehearsed weaknesses in the High Court's use of the concept [of proximity] stem from those moments where they have misunderstood or misapplied it and where a reading of Levinas might have, and might still, help' (Manderson, *Proximity*, p. 142).
20. For an elaborated critique along these lines, see Stone, 'Law, Ethics and Levinas's Concept of Anarchy', p. 99. See also Baxi, 'Judging Emmanuel Levinas?'.
21. Levinas, *Otherwise than Being*, p. 100.
22. This doctrine is traceable all the way back to *Donoghue v. Stevenson* [1932] UKHL 100, and finds its modern statement in *Caparo Industries plc v. Dickman* [1990] UKHL 2. The test was loosened somewhat by the House of Lords in *Page v. Smith* [1995] UKHL 7, where it was held that the precise type and extent of harm flowing directly from the defendant's actions need not be reasonably foreseeable, as long as the defendant could reasonably foresee the risk of some form of injury resulting from their actions.
23. Manderson, *Proximity*, p. 112 and generally pp. 107–18.
24. Ibid., p. 193.
25. See: Waldron, *The Right to Private Property*; Penner, *The Idea of Property in Law*; Macpherson, *The Political Theory of Possessive Individualism*.
26. A good recent example of this trend concerns the mechanism by which one can, or could, gain title to land via adverse possession. The practical scope for this was reduced massively by the 2002 Land Registration Act. Moreover, practices of adverse possession have more recently become criminalised by the Legal Aid, Sentencing and Punishment of Offenders Act 2012.
27. For a prescient analysis of this tendency, see Davies, 'Queer Property, Queer Persons'.
28. Locke, *Two Treatises of Government and A Letter Concerning Toleration*, pp. 111–21.

29. Kant, *The Metaphysics of Morals*, pp. 82–90.
30. Hegel, *Philosophy of Right*, pp. 57–84.
31. E.g. Radin, 'Property and Personhood'.
32. E.g. Cooper, 'Opening Up Ownership'; Keenan, *Subversive Property*.
33. Levinas, *Totality and Infinity*, p. 166.
34. Levinas, *Otherwise than Being*, p. 74.
35. Levinas, *Totality and Infinity*, p. 171.
36. Ibid., pp. 158–9.
37. Levinas, *Totality and Infinity*, pp. 154–6.
38. See 'Letter on Humanism' and 'Building, Dwelling, Thinking', both published in Heidegger, *Basic Writings*.
39. For a sustained comparison of Heidegger and Levinas's conceptions of dwelling, see Gauthier, *Martin Heidegger, Emmanuel Levinas and the Politics of Dwelling*.
40. Derrida, *Adieu*, p. 21. Original emphasis.
41. Levinas, *Totality and Infinity*, p. 171.
42. Ibid., p. 176.
43. Radin, 'Market-Inalienability'.
44. For an analysis of hospitality in both Levinas and Derrida, and its connection to our conceptions of property, see Aston and Davies, 'Property in the World'.
45. For example, Davies, 'Queer Property, Queer Persons', p. 346.
46. Burggraeve, 'The Good and Its Shadow', p. 96.
47. Emmanuel Levinas, 'The Prohibition of Representation and "The Rights of Man"', and 'The Rights of the Other Man', both in *Alterity and Transcendence*; 'The Rights of Man and the Rights of the Other', in *Outside the Subject*; 'The Rights of Man and Good Will', in *Entre Nous*.
48. Levinas, *Alterity and Transcendence*, p. 127.
49. Levinas, *Outside the Subject*, p. 96.
50. Ibid., p. 95.
51. Ibid., p. 96.
52. E.g. Arendt, *The Origins of Totalitarianism*, p. 299–300. The implications of this exclusionary nature of human rights as juridical instruments will be taken up again in Chapter 6.
53. Levinas, *Outside the Subject*, p. 91.
54. Ibid., p. 98.
55. Levinas, *Alterity and Transcendence*, p. 149.
56. Levinas, *Outside the Subject*, p. 97.
57. Quoted in English in Topolski, 'Relationality as a "Foundation" for

Human Rights', p. 2. The original source is Levinas's conversations with François Poirié, published in French as *Emmanuel Lévinas: Qui Êtes-Vous?*

58. Levinas, *Outside the Subject*, p. 92. As Roger Burggraeve's reading of Levinas puts it, 'a whole array of establishments, structures, and agencies' are necessary to achieve the form of social justice that Levinas describes (Burggraeve, *The Wisdom of Love in the Service of Love*, p. 142).

59. Simmons, *Human Rights Law and the Marginalized Other*, pp. 85–106.

60. Simmons draws parallels with Derrida's insistence that 'wholly other is totally other', whose 'desertified' construction of alterity goes even further in eliding political normativity (ibid., p. 89). See Derrida, *The Gift of Death*. The phrase is revisited in *The Politics of Friendship*, p. 232.

61. Levinas, *Outside the Subject*, p. 97.

62. Davidson, 'The Rights of the Other', p. 184.

63. Douzinas, *The End of Human Rights*, p. 355.

64. Ibid., p. 380.

65. E.g.: Tiemersma, 'Ontology and Ethics in the Foundation of Medicine'; Clifton-Soderstrom, 'Levinas and the Patient as Other'; Nortvedt, 'Levinas, Justice and Healthcare'.

66. Suffering receives brief attention in both *Totality and Infinity* and *Otherwise than Being*, and a fuller exposition in the essay 'Useless Suffering', in *Entre Nous*, pp. 78–87.

67. Conklin, *The Phenomenology of Modern Legal Discourse*, p. 45.

68. Diamantides, *The Ethics of Suffering*, p. 38.

69. Ibid., p. 40.

70. Ibid., p. 87.

71. Some have, for this reason, criticised Levinas for apparently helping sustain Western philosophy's pervasive anthropocentricism. See Matthew Calarco, 'Faced by Animals', p. 119.

72. Levinas, *Otherwise than Being*, p. 44.

73. Levinas, 'The Paradox of Morality', p. 172.

74. E.g., *Basic Philosophical Writings*, p. 12.

75. Calarco, 'Faced by Animals'.

76. Levinas, *Difficult Freedom*, pp. 151–3.

77. Ibid., 153.

78. Crowe, 'Levinasian Ethics and Animal Rights'.

79. Levinas, 'The Paradox of Morality', p. 172. Also cited in Crowe, 'Levinasian Ethics and Animal Rights', p. 321.

80. For a more skeptical reading of Levinas's position on the animal based largely on his 'Paradox of Morality' interview, see Calarco, 'Deconstruction is Not Vegetarianism'. In particular, at p. 184: 'For Levinas, the animal is without *human* ethics; the ethical relation with the animal is based on the "prototype" of human ethics – the human remains always and everywhere the measure of the animal'.
81. Douzinas and Warrington, 'Law and Ethics in Postmodernity'. See also the similar chapter, 'A Well-Founded Fear of the Other', in *Justice Miscarried*, pp. 211–41.
82. E.g. Pugliese, 'The Reckoning of Possibles'; Metselaar, 'When Neighbours Become Numbers'; Loughnan, 'Detention and Dwelling'.
83. Douzinas and Warrington, 'Law and Ethics in Postmodernity', p. 129.
84. Pugliese, 'The Reckoning of Possibles', p. 31.
85. Derrida, *Of Hospitality*, p. 45.
86. Here it is worth revisiting Levinas's comments on the 1982 massacre at the Shatilla refugee camp, in which he alluded to the enmity of the Palestinian neighbour for the Israeli subject. It is hard to imagine that this comment was devoid of a personal politics. But insofar as it reflects a political rather than ethical position, it reveals the limits of a normativity of hospitality that might be derived from his work. The third forces us to make a difficult set of decisions, which may entail making enemies. It opens up complexity in the relation of the ethical and the political, in which the latter extends beyond imperatives of hospitality, and can contain violence. Levinas reveals the same dynamic to this relation, but in the other direction, when he spoke of the necessity of the SS officer having a face (*Entre Nous*, p. 200). The violence and enmity of their political existence does not prevent them from signifying ethically. But, presumably, this in turn does not command that one should be politically hospitable.

Part III
Ethics Against the Law

5

The Law of the Same: Levinas and the Biopolitical Limits of Liberalism

Having provided an overview of the various ways we might read Levinas in relation to law, and the issues they raise, it is time to put forward the substantive argument of the book. This is the first of two concluding chapters making the argument that Levinas is best read as someone who offers us the possibility of thinking about ethics as perpetual critique of the law, rather than as a legal theorist. In other words, instead of using his work to think about how we inject ethics into law or unveil law's ethical foundation, his philosophy provides resources to understand how the ethical structure of the encounter with the other arises as a persistent challenge to the law's ontological fixity. A chief reason for taking his theory in this direction is the necessity of resisting an idealistic depiction of the opportunities for ethical exposure within legal processes, and of placing Levinas's insights into conversation with critical theories of law's operation, its complicity with power, and its relation with the political. Readings of Levinas often tend, quite understandably, to loosely follow a discernible, although by no means unqualified, liberal outlook in Levinas's own work. Such implicit liberalism should be placed into conversation with some of the more prominent critiques of liberal modes of governance in critical theory, which can be gathered under the category of biopolitics. Analyses of biopolitics illuminate a tendency for the contemporary exertion of power, including through legal frameworks, to be justified not by a series of political, moral or, indeed, ethical ideas, but through a profoundly depoliticised matrix of factual claims to what individual and collective life is. To put this in Levinasian terms, power is grounded with reference to a totalised determination of being.

The previous two chapters considered how law, in its moments of justice, seeks to give a form of ontological expression to our pre-originary ethical relations. Whilst a Levinasian jurisprudence such as this represents a legitimate although rather utopian aspiration, it is argued that a biopolitical-legal paradigm, by its very nature, obstructs the irruptive exposure to the ethical demand that a Levinasian jurisprudence requires. However, what one also finds in Levinas if one pursues this thread are a set of resources that are profoundly antibiopolitical, in their resistance to the determination of governmental norms of being. To take seriously the phenomenon of biopolitics makes our hope for an ethical openness within the familiar structures and norms of law remote, and also redoubles the importance of reading Levinas as generating ways to understand life, and its ethical condition, in its critique of law.

Levinas and Liberal Theory

First, however, we need to acknowledge the elephant in the room: Levinas frequently wrote in favour of the liberal state. Despite resisting the idea of the political as a consensus of aggregated individuals, he neverthe-less found something enduring in liberal ideas. The initial task therefore involves tracing how far his adoption of the political ideas of liberalism extends, and how centrally it sits with his core philosophical framework. Whilst subject to inexorable internal debates, conventional liberal juris-prudence does have a core of reasonably settled meaning, holding that the function of law is to allow people maximum freedom to pursue their own ends, moral or economic, as far as possible without being inconsist-ent with others' freedoms and some basic regulatory principles of justice.[1] Such a vision informs us that the principal role of law is not to assert any particular set of values (beyond the values inherent in liberal ideas, such as liberty), but should instead provide a platform through which competing values can co-exist in the same political community. To see the immediate parallels with Levinas, take the analysis of adjudication that he posits in *Otherwise than Being* and 'Peace and Proximity'. In these pieces legal adjudication demands a decision in the name of reason and in the presence of the other and the third. Such judgment must pass through the aporetic passage from singular ethical duties to general, intel-ligible principles. The process of comparison and prioritisation, central to his idea of justice, seeks to effectuate a maximally responsive outcome in which responsibility is assimilated by a form of calculation within a matrix of reciprocal and 'essentially egalitarian' law.[2] The other must be reduced to the same. As discussed earlier, Levinas cannot determine the precise content of legal norms, with the exception, of course, of the neces-sary primacy he gives to broader imperatives such as freedom, responsibil-ity and fraternity (values arguably liberal in nature) which are expressed by the process of adjudication itself. Unlike classical liberal jurisprudence, and as explored in the previous chapter, the Levinasian outlook requires the judge to adopt a more radical position, possibly to the extent that they are cast in the role of the rebel. Their job requires them to apply the law in all its generality, but due to an exceptional process of ethical exposure, interpretation and judgment, justice may still demand the rupture of the prevailing legal framework in a gesture of fidelity to the other, effacing existing law in a commitment to justice. Yet this description of comparison and prioritisation does bear some formal resemblance to the liberal idea of justice as mediating between individuals' needs. Furthermore, leaving aside the precise nature of legal interpretation, Levinas suggests that the law has an important role to play in creating a broader social framework that facilitates the maximal recognition of people's ethical drives, duties and the freedom they find therein. The most significant example to be recalled here is Levinas's later writings on human rights. Additionally, both *Existence and Existents* and *Totality and Infinity* could be read alongside classical social contract theorists, positing a bleak and chaotic elemental world in the *there is*, out of which the subject discovers itself in its relation with others, and ultimately in the necessity of state law in mediating our desires and our responsibilities.[3]

Levinas's politics have to be responsive to the manner in which responsibility is felt uniquely and structures the subject's individuality. Levinas therefore both draws attention to and challenges our understanding of the individual and its freedom as a locus of political theory. The aggregated individual liberty of conventional liberal states would not satisfy Levinas, as it would not produce any sort of meaningful freedom but instead the lonely enchainment to one's own being. But reflected directly in some of his writings, such as those on rights, is the idea that law finds a type of liberal expression in the protection of the freedom we find in ethical responsibility. Fred Alford describes this compellingly as an 'inverted liberalism' in which the individual is prioritised 'not for the sake of the individual, but rather for the other'.[4]

These contortions of certain aspects of liberal jurisprudence must also be read in conjunction with Levinas's wider (although, as we will see, qualified) support for liberalism as a political doctrine, which has been the subject of much existing discussion. It is a discussion in part prompted by his own personal relation with politics, and the difficulty of reconciling some of his positions on philosophical ethics with the more expedient questions of lived political problems. In some lights, Levinas appears highly cynical about political frameworks in general. 'Politics left to itself', he tells us towards the end of *Totality and Infinity*, 'bears a tyranny within itself'.[5] Elaborating on these themes in a 1983 interview, he talked of the way in which there must be 'an element of violence in the state',[6] which, if left unchecked, means that state power tends towards totalitarianism. But even democratic regimes have an inherent violence: this is the necessary consequence of politics addressing itself to the multiplicity, and therefore expressing an ontological language of the said.

Recalling his references to the 'extraterritorial' dimension of the rights of the other, the state cannot become a totalised echo chamber; it must be opened onto its beyond. And for Levinas it is the liberal state in which there is potential for a workable but tense co-presence of ethics and politics in this fashion.[7] This is a state that is 'always concerned about its delay in meeting the requirement of the face of the other', committed to 'the rights of man'.[8] It is a 'state capable of extending beyond the state' in meeting these demands,[9] and must always be restless, never static in its pursuit of justice.[10] What distinguishes this form of state in particular is its capacity to surpass the governance of people through abstract institutional and legal categories, and to provide a platform for the extraterritorial demands of justice to be met, which Levinas felt would come from the work of its people rather than purely via the state's own self-justified power.[11] More concretely, it has been suggested that a number of empirical characteristics of the liberal state allow it to take such priority in Levinas's politics. Such a state permits a freedom of its people to criticise authority and incorporates a concern for fellow citizens into government via democratic process.[12] By now it probably comes as little surprise that, as Victoria Tahmasebi-Birgani has put it, the commentary on Levinas's political legacy can be interpreted as 'a continuation and a deepening of the liberal political tradition'.[13]

To interrogate this sort of claim further, we might need to ask additional questions about the way in which Levinas aligns our thinking with a tradition that conventionally prioritises the liberty of the individual. First, recalling Fred Alford's idea of 'inverted liberalism' above, to what extent does it make sense to talk of an individual in this inverted context? Levinas did not use the term 'individual' often, but it is clear that he approaches it critically. Revisiting the question of the role of the state, he describes the challenge of how we 'reconcile the infinite ethical requirement of the face that meets me, dissimulated by its appearance, and the appearance of the other as an individual and as an object'.[14] To be recognised as an individual in the eyes of the state, as a citizen, is opposed to uniqueness. It mediates the intersubjective experience through ontological categories. But moreover, as we know, Levinas describes a constitutive tension between autonomy and heteronomy, between finitude and infinitude, in his depiction of subjectivity. Only a subject that has a sense of itself as its own finite entity can apprehend the constitutive and infinite debt that is owed to the other. As Levinas explains through his idea of substitution, the subjectivity of the subject, their 'individuality' if you will, is found in the other. Therefore, to slightly adjust Alford's formulation above, the prioritisation of the individual in Levinas's outlook may be for the sake of the other *and* the individual itself. Paradoxically, we find our autonomy and identity in the uniqueness of our indebtedness to the other.[15]

This leads into the second issue, which is to what extent one can talk about a liberal form of freedom in a Levinasian sense. In a conventional view, freedom is a freedom to pursue one's own drives and interests; it is a form of sovereignty of the self. If freedom is inverted, such as to mean finding oneself in one's responsibility rather than in isolation, and thereby in the unchaining of oneself from itself,[16] then we arrive at a further series of questions about how this can be reconciled with more familiar liberal principles. What does it mean for the state to facilitate our personal experiences of ethical bondage to the other? How can law provide a framework in which we realise our own subjectivity in ethics? Such a framework obviously cannot be centred on the protection of the subject's sovereign possession of individual rights and entitlements (which would revert to an entirely uninverted liberalism), but nor can it easily prescribe what we ought to do to be ethical, which is something singular, unique, pre-ontologically given. Law is excellent at defining, protecting and insulating the individual; it is less clear what role it can play in promoting a form of inverted personal freedom, derived from a radical ethics, without collapsing back into conventional liberalism. Levinas's later writings on rights, emphatic in their championing of the 'rights of the other' whilst holding back from a clear depiction of their practical application, give some illustration of the challenges in concretising this jurisprudence.

Liberal Biopolitics

Writing in a 1990 preface to a 1934 article on 'Hitlerism', Levinas asked the reader to consider 'if liberalism is all we need to achieve an authentic dignity for the human subject'.[17] He was referring to how we protect ourselves against the historical violence of a politics of being for the sake of being (in that specific case, National Socialism). Annabel Herzog makes a crucial point in her commentary on this piece, supplementing Levinas's own equivocation on the political ideas he evidently valued. She argues that a political theory centred around the idea of an individual, even one that is constituted by alterity in Levinas's sense, tends to promote the expression, flourishing and *conatus essendi* of those individuals. Herzog posits that, on the contrary, the state must exist not for those represented by the state itself, but for the other: 'The *important* part of politics is precisely what is not politics itself, its counterpart, the absentees'.[18] The state must therefore go beyond facilitating the private ethical responsibilities of its citizens, and must strive for those who do not even appear. Levinas had already alluded to this capacity in his various other references to the extraterritoriality of the liberal state, mentioned earlier. Yet his prevarication here, on whether liberalism really is 'all we need', is telling.

The literatures on biopolitics suggest not only that the apparatuses of modern liberal governance fail to serve those absentees, but also that they produce their very exclusion. We are therefore prompted to put Levinas in conversation with these writings, which perhaps more than any other trajectory of thinking reveal the ways in which liberalism both constructs and subordinates alterity as one of its constitutive functions, in a movement of double ontological violence. Such thinking shows how liberalism fails to do what Levinas precisely needs it to do if his scattered notes of support for the liberal state are to cohere with his philosophy; that is, to serve those who are outside the enfranchised terrain of political life.

From Foucault, to Agamben, to Esposito, not to mention the many prominent theorists who have followed their work, one cannot arrive at anything resembling a comprehensively unified theory of biopolitics.[19] But a number of key points can be taken from their respective frameworks, whose justification will be attempted over the coming pages. First, biopolitics concerns the management of life via factual or scientistic forms of understanding that lack the appearance of essential contestability that manifest in traditional political or moral ideas. Secondly, via what can be termed a logic of exceptionalism, biopolitics feeds off the constitutive construction of what is other to the acceptable political mode of life. In this way, biopolitics operates through the distinction between norm and exception. Thirdly, the (in)operation of law is essential to the practice of biopolitical governance. Law enables biopolitical practice both through its application and its withdrawal, through disciplinary frameworks, directly punitive measures, and by simply abandoning other life outside its sphere of protection. Finally, whilst biopolitics found a particular and heightened expression in histories of genocide and particularly Nazism, it continues to operate generally in a converse form within Western liberal societies today.

As good a place as any to start is with Foucault – admittedly not a natural bedfellow for Levinas, and so we need to avoid making the mistake of assuming a direct translatability between their theoretical methods. Foucault appears an obvious target for Levinas's cynicism about anti-humanism[20] whilst, conversely, positing a model of agentic subjectivity seems antithetical to Foucault's own philosophical objectives.[21] But Foucault will help make the general argument about biopolitics as an ontologisation of governing life. Ontologisation here assumes the narrower Levinasian notion of the assimilation of otherness into circumscribed orders of meaning – connections, hierarchies, dichotomies of meaning – that form a totality that can be described as 'the same'.

The famous basic definition of what Foucault first called 'biopower' in the initial volume of the *History of Sexuality*, as the 'power to foster life or disallow it to the point of death',[22] came to be elaborated and developed extensively in his lectures at the Collège de France. Foucault observed how, since the middle of the eighteenth century, we saw in Europe a new political concern with management of the population. It is at this point that matters concerning reproduction and birth rate, health, death and lifespan become part of an economy of knowledge that is critical to the political and economic governance of society within modernity.[23] Foucault notes how the regulatory management of life, based on these new objects of knowledge, came to influence all manner of practices around housing and the urban environment, health and hygiene, education, work, and so on.[24] In this context, such knowledge allows for the generation of norms – but it is crucial to understand here that a norm does not refer to a moral or political practice to which a participant reflectively and consciously subscribes. It is a norm in the sense of an understanding of a normal pattern or distribution of social phenomena, which allows different, deviant phenomena to be perceived as so and sought to be brought into line.[25]

At the end of his 1975–6 lectures, Foucault turns his attention to the issue of racism. This is of particular importance for us because it is where Foucault illustrates most starkly how otherness is interpreted in biopolitical society. That the normativised mode of living produces a conception of the 'normal' is a necessary consequence of the way in which norms are derived from matrices of knowledge. Norms do not describe particular conceptions of ideal or virtuous life, but instead lay out basic and apparently neutral ideas of what it means to live. The corollary of this is, of course, that the production of anything outside this conception of normality is coded as abnormal. The appearance of anything other to the norm as being degenerate in this way is the definition, for Foucault, of biological racism. This is a type of racism that is not based on enmity or moral disagreement with others' lifestyles, but, much more powerfully, on seeing others as living outside the threshold of a normal life and as a threat to that life.[26]

When Foucault refers (briefly) to 'the other' as the figure whose death in the practices of racism 'will make life in general healthier',[27] he is of course not utilising the term in the transcendent form devised by Levinas. It is necessary to emphasise again the challenge of translation between these thinkers. But the dissonance between these two expressions of alterity strikes precisely to the point that needs to be made, which is that in the biopolitical society otherness becomes constructed and assimilated in a particular way. Whilst the racial or otherwise abnormal other manifests beyond the interior normative framework, they are nevertheless ontologised within a graspable structure of knowledge. What we see here, therefore, is a set of practices that operate to close off the transcendent aspect of the human encounter, such that difference is immediately mediated through Levinas's understanding of ontology, as a reduction from the other to the same. What is 'other' for Foucault, as an excluded form of unacceptable life, is part of the economy of the same in Levinas's framework. Whilst Foucault's racial other manifests as different to us, in Levinasian terms it expresses a sameness deriving precisely from its construction through the ontological dichotomy of normal/abnormal, for example via the structure of racism. The Foucauldian abnormal other emerges as an object of knowledge in an economy of the same, rather than its transcendent radical alterity. The significance of the specifically biological construction of this difference is that the alterity it produces appears as rooted in immutable, material fact.

Moving on, by understanding the norm as an aspect of knowledge rather than a traditionally political or moral idea, one can appreciate Foucault's concern with practices of what he describes as security, which allow power to be deployed and justified via a rhetoric of necessity. Security presumes and reinforces an idea of reality that, through a variety of prescriptive and prohibitive measures, effectuates a natural 'letting be'.[28] The appearance of naturalness is reinforced by apparatuses of security stimulating fear of what is deemed a threat to the freedom of normal life, namely those abnormal others.[29] Freedom therefore takes on an ideological status, meaning the practices of security assume a façade of urgency in protecting the basic continued existence of the internal life of the population. Foucault posits this structure of governance as liberalism.[30] This definition refers just as much to liberalism's economic structure as its social, as biopolitical apparatuses of security and governance have the effect of facilitating a political economy that appears to be guided by the natural expression of the free market. Capitalism needs a mode of operation whereby people understand themselves as free, decisional market actors whilst internalising their role as constituent parts of an apparently neutral economic order.[31] As Thomas Lemke has emphasised, biopolitical practices cannot be regarded as monopolised by the state, and find multifarious articulations within the private sector,[32] something we can readily see, for example, in the private management of spaces of biopolitical exceptionalism such as immigration detention centres. Foucault therefore allows us to starkly challenge the notion that liberal apparatuses are defined, as Levinas hoped, by their capacity to be opened to the rupture of the ethical encounter and the possibilities of justice that arise therein. Being predicated on a 'letting be', on the protection of a normalised conception of being, against which difference is dichotomised and cognised as abnormality, biopolitical liberalism works in precisely the opposite fashion, assimilating and ontologising otherness.

Meanwhile, Agamben draws a distinction between *bios* and *zoe*, acceptable political life and abandonable bare life, which, he argues, is woven into the very structure of sovereignty. Following threads left by Carl Schmitt, he claims that sovereignty has an irreducibly paradoxical character in that it must be both outside and inside the legal order.[33] It must give meaning and validity to the legal structure, yet itself lacks the authorisation that it provides to law.[34] From this position sovereignty delineates the boundaries of the juridical through a logic of the exception, constituting what is included with reference to what is excluded. Bare life, exemplified in the embodied figure of *homo sacer*, is that which is produced as the excluded condition of *bios*. Bare life can be abandoned, killed without sanction, lacking law's protection by virtue of its exclusion. Yet this exclusion is never absolute; it always rests in a zone that is both inside and outside. Sovereignty therefore has an intrinsically biopolitical tendency, that Agamben argues finds its paradigmatic expression in modernity. At its limit-point, the production of otherness in Agamben's study of Auschwitz takes on the figure of the *Muselmann*, the survivor of total subjugation who is not excluded from a conception of humanity, but inhabits an indistinction between inhuman and human.[35]

Auschwitz represents the nadir of genocidal biopolitics owing to the way in which particular forms of life, whether racialised as Jewishness or traced upon other lines of difference such as sexuality, are reduced to constructions of pure biological materiality, and coded as direct (and often explicitly biological) threats to the security of the German population. Moreover, Agamben claims that today we see a generalised paradigm of 'the camp' in which governance tends towards the adoption of the logic of Auschwitz, not only by making norm and exception a central concern of the political, but also multiplying instances in which the two become indistinct.[36] This transformation is not so much a product of liberal ideology as it is the loss of a distinct meaning to liberalism, once governance becomes orientated around questions of bare life.[37] The Nazi state and the contemporary liberal state represent different expressions of the same preoccupation of modern sovereignty with life itself. This summary of Agamben is unremarkable, but the key point to take is that such a preoccupation inevitably rests on the ontologisation of otherness within a dichotomous relation with the norm. Again, one sees a logic in which alterity is rendered graspable and present in order to effect its constitutive 'exclusion' from the productive life of the political community. Furthermore, a pervasive conflation of norm and exception means that this exertion of power is not reducible to a simple delineation of essential territorial boundaries of identity between inside and outside.[38] The state applies its biopolitical logic so as to cut across itself.[39]

For Agamben, then, the generalisation of the camp in liberal democratic states flows from the structure of sovereignty, and the intensification of its logic within modernity. Foucault, on the other hand, makes a sharper distinction between the direct application of the sovereign right to kill, deployed to excess by the Nazis, and the biopolitical practices of producing and regulating life. Roberto Esposito attempts to make sense of this difference. He argues that Nazi and contemporary liberal variants of biopolitics can be understood as incorporating opposing conceptions of freedom, the former devoted to the totalitarian constriction of freedom whilst the latter devoted to multiplying freedom through the figure of the individual as an object of knowledge.[40] Yet by formulating freedom via an intense negativity, in which the idealistic individual subject must be protected from others, this latter model represents a perverse denigration of freedom itself.[41] But, again, the point to be emphasised from the brief review of, likely familiar, theoretical literatures is that one can delineate a distinct set of relationships between governance and alterity. Such relationships are depicted as essential to those apparatuses of governance in modernity: the reduction of the other to the same, in which otherness becomes ontologised as otherness, for the sake of the same.

A couple of observations can be made to tie these frameworks back to Levinas. First, and as already mentioned, the alterity constructed via biopolitical practice is rendered graspable and knowable, thereby foreclosing the Levinasian experience of ethical exposure. Indeed, this is the very condition of its possibility. Knowledge, for Levinas, cannot express the full otherness of the other, which is cognised only insofar as it appears upon a plane of immanence.[42] There is a crucial question of visibility, or perhaps more accurately of representation, here. Spaces of bare or abandoned life tend to be hidden or concealed, allowing established, often bureaucratic, structures of meaning to be superimposed over the suffering of the other. The presence of the other as a knowable, abnormal threat covers over the infinitude of their alterity. When Levinas warns of the institutional violence of the blindness of the 'civil servant' to the other's suffering,[43] he anticipates the way that biopolitical power is typically exerted without affective exposure, enabling to a greater extent its reductive, assimilative impact.[44] Secondly, and relatedly, as all of our theorists on biopolitics should agree, the marginalised life of biopolitical society is constitutive of its healthy corollary. Biopolitical techniques allow otherness to be presented as part of the way in which we are channelled into understanding ourselves. I am a citizen *because* I am not an extremist; my gender is normal *because* I am not transsexual; I am white *because* I am not black. Furthermore, the appearance of difference as exceptional supports the firm economy of sameness that operates specifically in the construction of acceptable interior life. The difference between normal and abnormal life serves to entrench the homogeneity of the life of the former whilst the latter takes on an exceptional quality that ensures it does not count. This is precisely the reason why the law, as well as other apparatuses, has an ability to kill or abandon other life. In other words, whatever difference manifests in this ontological horizon manifests precisely for the sake of sameness. This contemporary configuration of the political and legal spheres therefore has an automated defence against radicalism, recalling Slavoj Žižek's claim that the modern condition is 'the radical obliteration of Difference, of the antagonistic gap'.[45]

Law and the Biopolitical Construction of Alterity

It is necessary to go beyond the primer on the basic theses of biopolitics, above, and justify the claim that this construction and assimilation of otherness via biopolitical practice is a phenomenon intrinsically linked to law. Whilst this is relatively straightforward in reading Agamben, it has at times been assumed that Foucault's thinking had little application to law or, more specifically, that it operated to de-prioritise law within historical practices of power, even in the context of sovereignty.[46] Yet, as Mariana Valverde has noted, this outlook can barely be sustained since the publication of his lectures at the Collège de France in the late 1970s and early 1980s.[47] It has been suggested that what Foucault sought to decentre as a site of power was not the law *per se*, but the monopoly of the juridical form of law as the direct expression of monolithic sovereign power.[48] François Ewald emphasises a further distinction between the juridical and the norm, the latter of which continues to find plentiful expression in law, and which of course is at the heart of the normal/abnormal construction of alterity. The instruments of law, its 'constitutions, codes, laws ... must all refer back to what functions in society as a common standard, a normative and objective basis for judgment'.[49] In other words, such legal instruments refer back to the norm in its productive role, conditioning social and individual practices in conformity with one another (and whose productive effect can therefore be distinguished from the prohibitive role of sovereign juridical power). As Foucault puts it himself, demonstrating that he sees law as expressive but not exhaustive of normativity, law may 'carry out a codification in relation to the norm' which itself is developed 'from and below a system of law'.[50] Sovereign power is not reducible to law for Foucault, yet law is still a necessary apparatus in which sovereignty can find its continued expression through biopolitical strategies.[51]

We can look at some concrete legal examples of how otherness might become filtered through this reductive logic of the norm. In some contexts, alterity is constructed as a threat to the extent that it becomes a target for direct sanctions. As Ben Golder notes, the direct and prohibitive biopolitical impact of the criminal law is exemplified well by the historic illegality of homosexuality, in which an abnormal modality of life is met with the law's full punitive power.[52] In a similar vein, consider also the infamous criminal case of *R* v. *Brown*,[53] in which a group of men failed to persuade the House of Lords that their consent should be a valid defence to offences concerning their private sadomasochistic practices. The judgment of the case unreservedly constructs their behaviour as deviant, not merely in relation to the sadomasochistic acts but also their homosexual nature, which itself becomes constructed as degenerate and diseased, explicitly opposed to the healthy normality of heterosexual behaviour.[54] Such deviancy was contrasted explicitly against one participant's subsequent 'normal heterosexual relationship', as it was described in the Court of Appeal.[55] Several of the group appealed to the European Court of Human Rights on the basis that the domestic ruling contravened their Article 8 right to a private and family life under the European Convention. The appeal failed, however, on the basis that it was 'necessary in a democratic society' for the state to be able to interfere with such rights in the interests of health.[56] The case is therefore indicative of the law's propensity to uphold a conception of interior, healthy life by coding alternative practices as dangerous. That the consent of the parties between each other was insufficient to escape conviction signals their perceived threat to society at large and the irrelevance of their individual autonomy. Finally, not only has the law interpreted abnormality via the direct application of traditionally punitive sanctions, but also via corrective biological procedures applied to those convicted of same-sex offences. Most notably, the UK has a history of sanctioned use of hormone therapy designed to lower libido amongst offenders, potentially to the extent of impotence.[57]

Law expresses a biopolitical function as much by its withdrawal as its application. For example, still in the context of the criminal law's construction of sexuality, Golder has also traced the historical phenomena of successfully defending murder charges by arguing that the defendant acted in a panicked response to a same-sex sexual advance.[58] In such scenes one sees the law extricating itself from the defence of victims who exhibit a particular mode of living, abandoning them to a lawless zone of non-protection. In such cases the law operates through its very *inoperation*. The capacity for marginalised life to be abandoned is illustrated in further contexts of killing and torture. For example, Foucault's position on racism in particular prompts us to consider the biopolitical dynamics of the phenomenon of racialised police violence. Political tensions over fatalities of ethnic minorities at the hands of police officers in the US have become heightened in the last few years. Concerns reflect not merely the disproportionate death-rate (in 2015, 26.5 per cent of those killed by police in the US were black, whilst representing only 12.6 per cent of the US population in the last census),[59] but also the apparent lack of legal accountability. The high-profile deaths of Michael Brown, Eric Garner and Tamir Rice are united by the notably minor nature of their actions suspected to be criminal (in the case of Rice, a twelve year-old, the firearm he was suspected of wielding was a plastic toy). What is most significant for our purposes is not so much the law's deployment of potentially lethal force, but its failure to restrain such force being exerted, or to offer meaningful processes of justice subsequently. Law is seen to withdraw its protection from victims of violence, which in this context is increasingly subjected to racial critique. One cannot avoid recognising the directly anti-biopolitical significance of the slogan that arose in the wake of these cases that 'black lives matter'.

Similarly, consider the police killing of Jean Charles de Menezes in the UK, for which no individual was criminally prosecuted and for which the Metropolitan Police only eventually faced punishment via a fine under the Health and Safety at Work Act 1974. De Menezes was shot inside Stockwell London Underground Station in July 2005, having been mistakenly identified as a terrorist suspect (he was in fact an electrician, on his way to work). Indeed, perhaps the most significant biopolitical construction of otherness as an exceptional threat to the norm in the contemporary political scene is that of the terrorist. Since 2001, the UK has witnessed an enormous proliferation in anti-terror laws that have had the cumulative effect of launching a deep assault on civil liberties. These have entailed the erosion of *habeas corpus*,[60] the curtailing of public speech that is deemed extremist or otherwise dangerous,[61] and restricting the photography of public buildings and police officers.[62] Whilst such measures cut across the social terrain, specific sites of exceptionalism have arisen in Guantanamo Bay in Cuba, Abu Graib prison in Iraq, and Belmarsh Prison in south London. Guantanamo is the exemplar, whereby detainees effectively inhabit a legal non-space, being denied legal representation or trial, often held without charge, all whilst being classified as 'unlawful enemy combatants' – a phrase that has no effective legal meaning.[63] The spaces and technologies of the post-9/11 West reveal a heightened political concern to manage life that is deemed acceptable whilst abandoning (or killing) the life coded as the paradigmatic threat.[64]

The repeated deployment of a rhetoric of security in justification of these legal tactics recalls the dichotomy of freedom and danger that Foucault identifies as essential to liberalism. Such a dichotomy has also allowed for various ways in which law can detach itself from democratic procedure and due process. The Civil Contingencies Act 2004, for instance, allows temporary regulations to be passed directly by government ministers, including the amendment of existing legislation, in situations of military or terrorist threat to the security of the UK.[65] Such regulations may aim to protect the life and health of citizens, social infrastructure and economic activity, as well as private property. The recent Data Retention and Investigatory Powers Act 2014 enabled the security services access to twelve months of data on individuals' internet activity, demonstrating how little the outcry over the activities of the National Security Agency (NSA) in the US had impacted on the UK government's resolve to monitor private digital communications. Such measures, whilst often facing significant opposition from much of the public, are frequently sought to be justified by the protective language of crisis and necessity.[66]

Those who have faith in liberal modalities of jurisprudence to respond ethically to the other must confront these particular ways in which otherness is contorted and brought into presence. Biopolitical critique prompts us to understand these measures not as merely over-zealous attempts to address anomalous emergencies, but as embedded within the essential structure of modern, liberal governance. In particular, the freedom sought to be protected relies upon a dichotomisation of the norm and its degenerate, threatening counterpart. Of course, none of this is to argue that Levinas's ethics should ask the law to respond hospitably to genuinely violent extremists, for instance. Rather, it is to illustrate the way in which governance as a whole becomes colonised by a logic in which pre-given categories of knowledge are deployed such that the pairings of same and other, inside and outside, norm and exception, become dominant. This structure not only lacks ethical sensibility, but is precisely an *anti*-ethical gesture. Exposure to the provocation of the other's infinitude requires the assumption of a radical passivity. The biopolitical duality of norm and exception, on the other hand, incorporates and instrumentalises the exterior term. The health, stability and productivity of the norm must be placed into relation with its threatening opposite to be fully constituted. This is a structure, then, that displays a profound ontologically reductive effect, not only purporting to understand alterity within a totality, but also deploying that assimilation as a central component of its own operation. The filtering of alterity through this schema, the reduction of radical otherness to a term within an economy of the same, is essential to the biopolitical structure of the legal status quo.

This incorporation of otherness through objects of knowledge gestures us towards Levinas's 1984 essay 'Transcendence and Intelligibility'. Here, Levinas reveals the implications of knowledge operating as a pre-given frame through which alterity is thematised. It is not merely the case that knowledge functions as a reduction of the other to the same – this, as we know, is implicit in his ideas on the intelligibility of the said. Furthermore, knowledge allows for something to be perceived as different whilst ensuring that its alterity is assimilated through this reductive operation. Therefore, knowledge ensures that 'thinking relates itself to the other but the other is no longer other as such; the other is already appropriated, already *mine*'.[67] This is not to call for a nihilistic abandonment of knowing. On the contrary, what Levinas critiques in this passage is not knowing as such, but the practices in which the expression of being delivered by knowledge becomes its own justification. As he makes clear in *Totality and Infinity*, the critical essence of knowledge is its capacity to be put into question by the other that is not thematised in advance.[68] When knowledge abandons the critical edge of the other's teaching that could open it onto the new, its phenomenology becomes one of bringing the world to presence in a synchronic experience of totality.[69] Furthermore, this reductive function of knowledge must impact upon the rather rudimentary idea of law that Levinas put forward in his analyses of legal judgment. The basic adjudicatory format of law, articulated in *Otherwise than Being*, fails to fully evince its own implication within the frameworks of knowledge and the determination of being that assimilate the other's alterity. Insofar as biopolitical practices feed off and perpetuate a factual matrix of normal/abnormal, in which otherness is ontologised as one term of a dichotomy in the economy of the same, then we are prompted to reappraise the extent to which the contemporary legal tradition can open the irruptive processes of justice at the service of ethics.

Travellers and the Limits of Liberal Jurisprudence

To summarise the argument so far, the rather hopeful, liberal applications of Levinas to law need to be responsive to the phenomenon of biopolitics and its implications for ethical sensibility and the way in which otherness is interpreted in juridical practice. Having made the broad case for this somewhat cynical outlook, it should be helpful to illustrate its implications via an extended example. The position of travellers presents an exemplary ethical challenge to the law, and to liberal governance in general. It is hard to imagine another category of people within Western societies that express difference with such intensity and in such numbers (thought to be up to 12 million across Europe). There is even an argument to be made that travellers embody something akin to a remainder to the very logic of the nation state.[70] The sociologist Judith Okely has suggested, quite provocatively, that the original traveller populations were adherents to an ambulant lifestyle that began in the turbulence of the emergence of the modern state and of early capitalist political economy.[71] She proposes that many of those who lost their livelihoods in the processes of industrialisation simultaneously found new nomadic ways of living outside the social mainstream. In this sense, the nomadic lifestyle expresses not a migratory search for home, but an entire rejection of the order and sedentariness of the modern juridico-political order. This interpretation is, of course, highly speculative. What is clearer, however, is the wealth of anthropological research that allows us to understand that the travellers' difference is informed by a pervasive set of preferences within such communities for remaining unintegrated into conventional social structures.[72] The question of non-assimilative ethical responsiveness is therefore crucial in this context. Of course, there is an important limitation of what can be said about the alterity of the traveller, as seeking to intellectualise the otherness of a posited identity is an ontological gesture in itself. This limitation addresses the distinction between, on the one hand, the non-phenomenological signification of the other in the form of saying, and on the other hand, the thematic and graspable appearance of various identities we conceive as others on the political and social terrain of the said.

The historical legal position of travellers has never been particularly favourable. In Britain, as soon as travellers emerged as an identified social group in the sixteenth century they were subject to laws that allowed for their execution, and up until the nineteenth century were dealt with as social nuisances in the same manner as vagrants.[73] The Draconian nature of the law's position has, predictably, been tempered in more recent times. However, what we tend to see is a shift from the illegalisation of nomadic traveller culture to its attempted assimilation into dominant sedentary norms around housing, habitation and property ownership. Most notably then, legal questions have concerned the extent of protections for travellers' capacity to pursue their traditional mode of dwelling. The civil law rules on trespass have been supplemented by the provisions of the Criminal Justice and Public Order Act 1994, which turned the continued occupation of an unauthorised traveller site into a criminal offence.[74] Yet it is not only occupation of land subject to others' rights that is at stake. An entrenched policy of encouraging conventional leasing and ownership of homes[75] means that many travellers have sought to buy land on which to establish their own residential sites. Planning law has therefore become central to the travellers' legal status.

Planning decisions are part of a semi-juridical, semi-bureaucratic process by which a local planning authority seeks to implement its current 'development plan' for the immediate area.[76] Such a plan, drawn up by a local authority whilst being constrained by national policy, will contain a comprehensive scheme for future building and land use in the area. It will plan for the provision of education and healthcare, commerce and residential land use, as well as transport links and environmental preservation. The development plan is exemplarily biopolitical in the Foucauldian sense, in the manner that it presents an objective, dispassionate scheme for the management of a local population in an optimally healthy and productive manner. Copious literature has examined the way that urban planning constructs the community as a matrix of objects of knowledge, whose needs are conceived through discourses of practicality and necessity, rather than any form of overtly moral or ethical imperative, and seeks optimal regulation of the spatial flows of people and resources.[77] The development plan represents an effort to produce and secure a healthy, industrious and stable local population. That the typical traveller form of community life falls outside this normative structure is evidenced both by the entrenched historical inadequacy of local authorities' provision of traveller sites[78] and the fact that applications by travellers to establish sites on their own land are significantly less likely than average to succeed.[79]

Within the Levinasian register, the use of such pre-given structures of meaning around the development of the local environment risks a pervasive deference to an economy of the same. The disproportionately frequent rejection of travellers' planning applications signifies a form of ethical closure: the deference to an established normative framework in which alterity is framed via a set of knowledge claims about the necessary ordering of the wider community. One might think that the most significant opportunity for the meaningful recognition of different modes of living within a liberal model lies in the distribution of rights. Yet the difficulty of invoking rights in travellers' planning disputes is exemplified by the cases of *Buckley* v. *United Kingdom*[80] and *Chapman* v. *United Kingdom*.[81] In each, traveller appellants took a case to the European Court of Human Rights on the basis that a rejected planning application represented a breach of the Article 8 right to a private and family life under the European Convention. In both appeals, the court agreed that such rights had been interfered with by the state, but upheld the planning decisions on the basis that the state enjoys a broad margin of appreciation to balance individuals' rights with wider social concerns. To do so, the court invoked subsection (2) of the Article, which states that interference with a human right is permissible in situations of necessity and for reasons of

> national security, public safety or the economic well-being of the country, for the prevention of disorder or crime, for the protection of health or morals, or for the protection of the rights and freedoms of others.

Furthermore, in *Buckley*, the court made a specific point of holding that a local authority was in a better position 'to evaluate local needs and conditions'.[82]

It is likely unsurprising that the decisions were met with criticism for their failure to provide for the basic needs of traveller communities and to meaningfully recognise their difference from the social mainstream.[83] But what is more important for the present analysis is to understand the structure and significance of this form of legal reasoning. It is notable not merely that an international court charged with the responsibility for protecting the individual freedoms of some of the most socially disadvantaged people in society defers to the purportedly greater wisdom of the bureaucratic workings of the local council. Nor that, in consequence, this represents a supreme failure to be responsive to such a form of intense and vulnerable otherness. It is also the way in which this deference is justified. By appealing to the necessity of upholding the security and economic productivity of society, the biopolitical logic of this rights framework is laid bare. The protection of rights can readily be withdrawn in this sort of scenario, such that the normativised order of being can be preserved. One might wish for acknowledgement that the position of a traveller made homeless (or an outlaw) by a rejected planning permission application is undeniably less dire than the measures inflicted upon inmates of Guantanamo Bay. The latter is a significantly more severe illustration of the contemporary biopolitical terrain of law. But a case like *Buckley* or *Chapman* does also illustrate well the ideological component of liberal biopolitics, masking the differentiating of certain practices of life behind the tedium of dealing with one's local authority.

It could of course be argued that, rather than provoking us to take his work in other directions, this is precisely why we *need* Levinasian jurisprudence, and in particular his model of the rights of the other. Is the problem with the *Buckley* judgment that it is not Levinasian enough, that it fails to properly understand the need to protect alterity as part of the institutional fabric of a society that seeks to do justice to our unconditional responsibilities to each other? This argument is internally coherent, and returns us to the overarching contention of this chapter, that such a hope remains merely utopian for as long as we see such a Levinasian jurisprudence being implanted within a liberal governmental tradition. Whilst the other provokes an inclination towards an escape from the determination of being, the example considered here illustrates the capacity of contemporary human rights instruments to instead relate to the other as an abstracted, interchangeable person,[84] and in doing so assimilates alterity into a normalised conception of life. In other words, the human right, rather than guaranteeing a basic dignity and responsiveness to otherness, sets a limit on the otherness it recognises, ensuring that its protection applies to what is ontologised as the norm, and can be disapplied if not.

Law and the *There Is*

The problem that this chapter has sought to outline is the complicity of familiar legal frameworks with an ontological determination of human life. We can conclude by gathering some further thoughts on the resources Levinas provides to understand the phenomenon of biopolitics and the political instrumentalisation of ontology. We may start by contextualising the above against his much earlier writings before, and some might even say in anticipation of, biopolitics' other extremity, in Nazism. As Agamben notes, Levinas's brief 1934 text on Hitlerism represents one of, if not the, earliest published recognitions of the eventual biopolitical significance of National Socialism.[85] Levinas contrasts the idealism of conventional liberal thought, in which people are made to accord with an abstract idea of a rational legal entity, with the structure of Marxist theory, in which humankind is posited as a product of material forces. Marxism succeeds in recognising that consciousness is determined by being, and is not an experience of the pure, sovereign freedom of the self.[86] Hitlerism represents a political instrumentalisation of the latter view, reducing human existence to its corporeal form, negating any gap between the self and its materiality and denying any value that transcends this embodied understanding of being. As Agamben claims, the likely unspoken target of Levinas's critique here is Heidegger and his delineation of Dasein as tied to its own factual and historical emplacement.[87] It is this latter trajectory of thinking that allows the human to become regarded as bare life.

In 'Getting Out of Being By a New Path', the extended prefatory essay to *On Escape* that won Levinas's glowing approval, Jacques Rolland notes not only the enduring importance of the *there is* to Levinas's philosophy as a whole, but also its implicit centrality to the Hitlerism essay. It is with the idea of the *there is*, which came to persist throughout the lifetime of Levinas's work, that he frames the stark, oppressive nature of holding the subject to a determination of what merely *is*, without the encounter with transcendence that opens the experience of time, responsibility and freedom. Recalling the exposition in Chapter 2, the reign of the *there is* was painted in the bleakest of terms as the effect of being as the horror of the night,[88] as the emptying of subjectivity. The *there is* flattens the distinction between interior and exterior; its 'anonymous current of being invades, submerges every subject, person or thing'.[89] As Rolland understands, Levinas's pre-war work identifies, and indeed foresees, the consequences of a politics in which one's existence is riveted, or drowned by being. Levinas understood quite explicitly the divisive and indeed racist logic in such a politics that enchains the person to their biological existence. By drawing the connection between this capacity of the *there is* to reduce a being to their material being, and the Nazi production of various types of racial 'noncitizens',[90] Rolland therefore reveals the implicit analytic of biopolitics in Levinas's work. Indeed, when referring in the same context to 'the man who is designated as "other" and who, as such, is the racial enemy of the human species',[91] he illuminates at its boldest the very pressing correspondence of Levinas's thinking with Foucault's. Somewhat forgivably, despite revealing the consequence of the pervasive linkage of governance to a conception of being, Levinas had evidently not fully foreseen the manners in which liberalism could produce its own inverted biopolitics in contrast to its genocidal counterpart.

But Levinas also later rejected the idea that anti-humanism is an antidote to the collapse of the dignity of humankind that reverberates in the wake of Nazism. Just as the *there is* has the effect of dissolving the human experience, the anti-humanist project poses its own risk of desubjectification, or what he calls the 'disappearance' of subjectivity at the very moment that it becomes intelligible as an object of structuralist enquiry:[92] what Foucault might equally call subjectivity, but understood as the product of subjection and not the encounter with the transcendent.[93] Levinas forewarns of an 'order that is neither human nor inhuman'.[94] Anti-humanism lacks the resources that he considers necessary to restore human dignity. But we should ask to what extent, for instance, Foucault's melancholic depiction of the human disappearing 'like a face drawn in sand at the edge of the sea'[95] is really opposed to Levinas's cynicism about subjectivity's dissolution in the turn from human to thing. Levinas seems to suggest this line of thinking should be avoided because it fails to renew an idea of the human subject that he finds in his inverted 'humanism of the other', a humanism defined by ethical responsibility. But notwithstanding his notion of alterity, which remains entirely alien to Foucault's thinking, he has already accepted much of the essence of this anti-humanist critique by emphasising the desubjectifying effect of being, and its potential mobilisation within matrices of power. Levinas's disagreement, in this respect, concerns the nature of the cure, not the diagnosis.

If Levinas therefore understood quite acutely the embryonic structure of twentieth-century biopolitics, the task then becomes seeing how this can be further tied to our understanding of law in general terms. Once again, the difficulty we encounter here is the underdevelopment of direct thinking on law within his work. However, the *there is* makes a brief but crucial reappearance in the passages on judgment and justice towards the end of *Otherwise than Being*. Levinas writes of the way in which the *there is* asserts itself after the thematisation of the said that occurs in processes of adjudication. In other words, even acts of judgment in which the said is written in the exigencies of justice are destined to become a component of our experience of this anonymous and expansive terrain of being. Furthermore, whilst *Totality and Infinity* briefly alludes to the *there is* as a state of anarchy,[96] the same text further reveals its connection to law when it conceives the latter as a general order that reduces the subjective experience of singularity to an objectivity, and containing the potential for the 'tyranny of the universal and impersonal'.[97] Whilst being's essence may carry with it an ethical residue, it is, just like Lady Justice, blind, neutral and objective. The 'presenting' of the decision and the writing of law is precisely the synchronisation of other times into the present, of diachronic temporality to the now. This is the fate of all law, even in the alternating movement of law's justification and criticism that operate as the rhythm of justice. But moreover, when placed at the service of an economy of the same – that is, when operating within a specifically biopolitical model of governance – law not only resembles but also intensifies the *there is*. In other words, the *there is* does not represent the law's incidental fate, but its fullest expression. It is a law that seeks to regulate what is with respect to a mere measure of its being, rather than aspire to what is 'to come', what is opened by the other.

When law becomes complicit with immanentist forms of governance, it ceases to convey the appearance of serving any type of transcendent purpose. It ceases to go beyond itself for the sake of the other. Justice and ethical value are subjugated to security, safety and regulation. If it is true, as Douzinas has remarked, that Western law has an increasing modern tendency to form 'part of a hugely expanded and variegated administrative domain', which 'does not represent or pursue any inherent logic, overarching policy direction or coherent value system',[98] then the point is not that law detaches itself from the distinctive structures of capital, (neo)liberalism, individualism, and so on. Rather – and here we once again refer back to Foucault's understanding of liberalism – law achieves its legitimacy as a form of management that only intervenes in order to continue *letting be*. It therefore has a distinctly ideological apparatus, assuming its administrative appearance by allowing a particular normativisation of life to manifest as natural. Foucault's understanding of power over life incorporated the idea that the control that it exerted was 'indispensable' to capitalism, in that it facilitated the productivity of the labour force and allowed economic criteria to operate in governance.[99] Agamben's understanding of the contemporary state of exception is closely linked to the forms of power exerted in the hegemony of global free-market economics and neo-conservative politics. With Levinas, and at a deeper level, we are able to understand that once law elides the ethical interruption of its own ontological continuity, the contemporary legal milieu resembles one of superficially egalitarian equivalence, destroying the political life of the asymmetry and uniqueness at the heart of subjectivity and identity. In this particular picture, the legal relation with the other cannot be thought as originating in ethical experience. Rather, it is a relation with the alter ego, the abstract image, and therefore not a relation with another person at all. When transcendence withdraws in this way, people are left consigned to share only their profound loneliness in the reign of all-pervasive anonymity. The human is assimilated into a plane of immanence that sees subjectivity dissolved into a regulative equilibrium whose superficial claim to equality veils its closure of the transcendent, affective provocation of alterity. This is achieved simultaneously by the strategies of exceptional violence or abandonment directed at those deemed abnormal or threatening.

In *Totality and Infinity* the *there is* is characterised as the 'elemental' that cannot be possessed, such as the sea or the wind.[100] Its correspondence with law entails that people's behaviour becomes regulated by knowledge of the elements, as if stewarded by dispassionate meteorological reports. Law's movement aspires to no radically other state, appears unguided by an extrinsic goal, and is not caused by anything beyond itself; it simply reverberates what *is*. Norm corresponds with fact. When subjectivity is subordinated to the elements, it becomes lost. The shelter of the 'dwelling', the for-oneself of subjectivity that is the condition of the for-the-other of ethics, may be built into the elemental (for the elemental, the *there is* is all that *is*), but the elements always display the risk of 'submerging' the dwelling.[101] Thus, the *there is* opposes the uniqueness of the human subject. By determining human life as an object of knowledge, law effectuates its desubjectivation by legitimating – if necessary by physical or economic force – the idea that they are simply a point of singularity within the cartography of what merely is, and blurring, if not erasing, the line between the generality of the *there is* and the internality of the dwelling.

Levinas's own wager is that this dispersion of being's plenitude through the solidity of the legal said is always capable of being punctured, torn open by the demand of the other and, ultimately, the exigency of the just decision. This is the alternating pattern of which Levinas spoke, in which law's continuity is in a perpetual state of rupture and recuperation. But to be content with this picture requires an idealistic conception of law, one in which law is a mere formal tool at humankind's disposal for the articulation of compromise and mediation, comparison and prioritisation, of our radically irreconcilable ethical demands and desires. This chapter has sought to undermine the presumptions required by such a reading of law, arguing that we must confront, instead, the ideological capacity of liberal concepts to disguise their biopolitical structure, in which being is determined as a totality of the same. Levinas's ideas on law failed to work through law's propensity to become entwined with such an ontological determination, such that the ethical demand of alterity must be resituated outside and against the law.

Notes

1. Defining liberalism exhaustively is beyond the scope of this chapter, and hopefully the reader does not need its various internal debates to be rehearsed. In support of the base definition provided, see Dworkin, 'What Liberalism Isn't'; Rawls, *Political Liberalism*; Waldron, 'Theoretical Foundations of Liberalism'.
2. Levinas, 'Peace and Proximity', p. 143.
3. In particular, Levinas's discussion of the dwelling as a site in which labour and possession take meaning is redolent of Locke's own contribution to property theory, notwithstanding Levinas's imbuing of possession with responsibility rather than pure entitlement. (See Levinas, *Totality and Infinity*, pp. 158–74). On the affinities between Levinas and Locke, also see McDaniel, 'Garden-Variety Liberals'.
4. Alford, 'Levinas and Political Theory', p. 162.
5. Levinas, *Totality and Infinity*, p. 300.
6. Levinas, *Is It Righteous to Be?*, p. 167.
7. Levinas, 'The Rights of Man and the Rights of the Other', p. 123.
8. Levinas, *Entre Nous*, pp. 174–5.
9. Ibid., p. 175.
10. Levinas, 'Paradox of Morality', p. 175.
11. Levinas, *Is It Righteous to Be?*, p. 181.
12. Simmons, 'The Third', p. 99; Simmons, *An-Archy and Justice*, p. 75.
13. Tahmasebi-Birgani, 'Does Levinas Justify or Transcend Liberalism?', p. 524.
14. Levinas, *Entre Nous*, p. 177.
15. Simon Critchley negotiated this particular problem by nominating the (roughly Levinasian) subject as the 'dividual', a subject that is

simultaneously singular and divided, and, moreover, determined precisely by those seemingly contradictory qualities. Critchley, *Infinitely Demanding*, p. 11.

16. Levinas, *Otherwise than Being*, p. 124.
17. Levinas, 'Reflections on the Philosophy of Hitlerism', p. 63.
18. Herzog, 'Is Liberalism "All We Need"?', p. 219.
19. Notably, Agamben claims boldly to set out to 'correct' or 'complete' Foucault's position by going further than the basic biopolitical idea that power becomes concerned and orientated around life itself, holding that, furthermore, political life and bare life merge in a zone of indistinction (Agamben, *Homo Sacer*, p. 9). Esposito subsequently offers his own attempts at issuing a corrective to Foucault, claiming that a crucial 'immunitary' bio-logic 'eluded' Foucault's understanding of power and life (Esposito, *Bios*, p. 45).
20. See Levinas, 'Humanism and An-archy'.
21. However, see Gordon, 'Foucault's Subject'.
22. Foucault, *The History of Sexuality Vol. 1*, p. 138.
23. Foucault, *Society Must Be Defended*, p. 243. On healthcare specifically, see Foucault, 'The Politics of Health in the Eighteenth Century'.
24. Foucault, *Society Must Be Defended*, p. 251.
25. Foucault, *Security, Territory, Population*, pp. 62–3.
26. Foucault, *Society Must Be Defended*, p. 255. On the dichotomous relation of necessity in modern law with the abandonment of certain racialised constructions of life, see Ferreira da Silva, 'No Bodies'.
27. Ibid.
28. Foucault, *Security, Territory, Population*, p. 48.
29. Foucault, *The Birth of Biopolitics*, pp. 66–7.
30. Foucault, *Security, Territory, Population*, p. 48.
31. On the relation between Foucauldian biopolitics and political economy, see Vatter, 'Foucault and Hayek'.
32. Lemke, 'The Risks of Security'. See also Lemke, 'An Indigestible Meal?'.
33. Agamben, *Homo Sacer*, especially pp. 15–29.
34. In this respect, it differs from the reading of Foucault that sees sovereignty find its expression in governmental techniques that are not limited to law. E.g. Butler, *Precarious Life*.
35. Agamben, *Remnants of Auschwitz*.
36. Agamben, *Homo Sacer*, p. 170.
37. Agamben, *Homo Sacer*, pp. 121–2.

38. On the idea of a 'generalised border', see Vaughan-Williams, 'The Generalised Bio-Political Border?'.
39. Here, Foucault would agree directly, claiming that the biopolitical management of life is co-extensive with the 'sovereign right to kill anyone, meaning not only other people, but also its own people' (Foucault, *Society Must Be Defended*, p. 260).
40. Esposito, *Third Person*, p. 91.
41. Esposito, *Bios*, pp. 69–77.
42. Levinas, *Basic Philosophical Writings*, p. 151.
43. Ibid., p. 23.
44. Compare with Carl Schmitt's theory of the political being structured in constitutive relation to the enemy. Whilst this does entail a relation between interior political life and an other, it is a reductive relation in which alterity is mediated through the interior's ontological horizon (Schmitt, *The Concept of the Political*).
45. Žižek, *Did Somebody Say Totalitarianism?*, p. 238. This point also recalls the claim made by Jean-Luc Nancy and Philippe Lacoue-Labarthe that 'the political' withdraws once politics is reduced to an immanent form of regulation. As they put it themselves, 'the retreat [of the political] appears, then, first of all as the retreat of transcendence or of alterity' (Nancy and Lacoue-Labarthe, *Retreating the Political*, p. 126). By expunging difference into the idea of bare life, to which political life owes no engagement, biopolitical critique is exemplary of such concerns about the reduction of the political.
46. Hunt and Wickham, *Foucault and Law*; the interpretation is certainly understandable when one reads phrases of Foucault's such as '[t]he law always refers to the sword' (Foucault, *The History of Sexuality Vol. I*, p. 144), invoking the juridical law as an expression of the sovereign's power to take life away, which is distinguished from biopolitical management of life.
47. Valverde, 'Law Versus History', p. 138.
48. On this point generally, see Golder and Fitzpatrick, *Foucault's Law*. Compare with Hunt and Wickham, *Foucault and Law*.
49. Ewald, 'Norms, Discipline, and the Law', p. 159.
50. Foucault, *Security, Territory, Population*, p. 56; Similarly, see Jon Simons's reading of Foucault, which holds that 'moral-legal norms are colonized by the administrative and statistical norms determined by power/knowledge regimes' (Simons, *Foucault and the Political*, p. 45).

51. See Butler, *Precarious Life*, p. 95.

52. Golder, 'The Distribution of Death', pp. 107–10.

53. *R v. Brown* [1994] 1 AC 212.

54. For an extended analysis, see Stychin, 'Unmanly Diversions'.

55. *R v. Brown*, p. 235, per Lord Templeman quoting Lord Lane in the Court of Appeal Judgment (*R v. Brown* [1992] QB 491).

56. *Laskey v. United Kingdom* (1997) 24 Eur HR Rep 39. Article 8(2) allows for interference with the right when measured against the interests of the wider population.

57. The most notable case of this sort in the UK was that of the mathematician and wartime code-breaker, Alan Turing.

58. Golder, 'The Distribution of Death', pp. 103–7.

59. 'The Counted: People Killed by Police in the US', *The Guardian*, available at *http://www.theguardian.com/us-news/ng-interactive/2015/jun/01/the-counted-police-killings-us-database* (last accessed 1 September 2015); Sonya Rastogi et al., 'The Black Population: 2010', available at *http://www.census.gov/prod/cen2010/briefs/c2010br-06.pdf* (last accessed 6 January 2016).

60. Suspicion of terrorism allows for a person to be held for fourteen days without charge (Protection of Freedoms Act 2012 s. 57). Whilst the attempt to legalise indefinite detention under the Anti-Terrorism, Crime and Security Act 2001 proved short-lived due to its inconsistency with the European Convention on Human Rights, the introduction of control orders and, subsequently, 'terrorism prevention and investigative measures notices', have provided sweeping powers to restrict the individuals' liberty without the evidential threshold for criminal charges being met. See the Terrorism Prevention and Investigation Measures Act 2011.

61. Part 3 of the Police Reform and Social Responsibility Act 2011 introduced stringent restrictions on political protest in Parliament Square. Meanwhile, the Terrorism Act 2006 created offences related to speech deemed to encourage terrorism (ss 1–4).

62. Terrorism Act 2000, s. 58; Counter-Terrorism Act 2008, s. 76.

63. Judith Butler has noted the significance of Guantanamo's administration being distinctly bureaucratic rather than traditionally juridical (the decisions that lead to a person's indefinite detention are made by administrators with reference to policy guidelines, rather than any form of judicial process). Butler conceives law as part of the tactical apparatus of governmentality; that is, capable of being deployed as much by its withdrawal as its application.

Whether it is accurate to call this a foreshadowing of a 'lawless future', as she puts it, is debatable however (Butler, *Precarious Life*, p. 58).

64. For a comprehensive study, see Pugliese, *State Violence and the Exception of Law*.

65. Distinguished by reference to the nebulous threat of terrorism, this Act represents a contemporary equivalent of the Emergency Powers (Defence) Act 1939, which granted powers for the pervasive management of life in wartime Britain, and allowed certain breaches of emergency regulations to be punished by death.

66. In this sense, we observe the immunitary structure to freedom in modernity, posited by Esposito: the measures emerging to protect freedom turn back to denigrate that very freedom (Esposito, *Bios*, pp. 69–77).

67. Levinas, *Basic Philosophical Writings*, p. 151.

68. Levinas, *Totality and Infinity*, pp. 85–6.

69. Levinas, *Basic Philosophical Writings*, p. 152.

70. Stewart, 'The Puzzle of Roma Persistence', p. 84.

71. Okely, *The Traveller-Gypsies*, pp. 8–15. The travellers' relationship with the state's modern capitalist form is further illuminated by studies that have shown that many traveller groups enjoyed a more favourable existence in communist countries in Eastern Europe as compared to those same states' post-communist incarnations after the fall of the Berlin wall. See Pogany, *The Roma Café*, p. 97; Stewart, *The Time of the Gypsies*, p. 232.

72. E.g. Stewart, *The Time of the Gypsies*, p. 27. And generally Fraser, *The Gypsies*; Acton, *Gypsy Politics and Traveller Identity*. For example, within Roma traveller communities the term 'Gaje' is used to describe non-Gypsies, and carries a distinctly pejorative implication of untrustworthiness, improperness and pollution (Weyrauch and Bell, 'Autonomous Lawmaking', pp. 24–5). Breaching customary social and domestic codes may be framed as behaving as 'Gaje' would (Okely, *The Traveller-Gypsies*, p. 83). These points are significant because they illustrate how traveller lives are lived not simply in a physically different manner to the rest of society, but also that there are complex and deep-rooted symbolic codes that allow travellers to understand themselves as different.

73. Originally thought to be immigrants, travellers were the target of a series of Egyptians Acts in the sixteenth century. For a concise history of travellers' relationship with the law, including a more

expansive analysis of their biopolitical treatment today, see Stone, 'Biopolitics and Movement'.

74. Section 77. As an indicator of the policy being pursued at the time, the statute also relieved local authorities of their duty to provide dedicated authorised sites.

75. Hawes and Perez, *The Gypsy and the State*, p. 128.

76. As governed by the Town and Country Planning Act 1990 and the Planning and Compulsory Purchase Act 2004.

77. On this aspect of the spatial distribution of power in urban planning within Foucault's writing, see Foucault, *Security, Territory, Population*, pp. 17–20. More generally, see Ploger, 'Foucault's Dispositif and the City'; Flyvbjerg, 'Planning and Foucault'.

78. Cemlyn et al., *Inequalities Experienced by Gypsy and Traveller Communities*; Niner, *Local Authority Gypsy/Traveller Sites in England*.

79. Jones et al., 'Planning Law', p. 75; Brown and Niner, *Assessing Local Authorities' Progress*, p. 23. Raw data is available at *https://www.gov. uk/government/collections/planning-applications-statistics* (last accessed on 5 September 2015).

80. *Buckley v. United Kingdom* (1997) 23 EHRR 101.

81. *Chapman v. United Kingdom* (2001) EHRR 399.

82. *Buckley v. UK*, p. 129.

83. See, for example, Sandland, 'Developing a Jurisprudence of Difference'.

84. On this point in particular, see Diamantides, 'From Escape to Hostage', p. 200.

85. Agamben, *Homo Sacer*, p. 151.

86. Levinas, 'Reflections on the Philosophy of Hitlerism', p. 67.

87. Agamben, *Homo Sacer*, p. 152.

88. Levinas, *Existence and Existents*, p. 55.

89. Ibid., p. 52.

90. Rolland, 'Getting out of Being By a New Path', p. 32.

91. Ibid.

92. Levinas, 'Humanism and An-Archy', p. 48.

93. Foucault, 'The Subject and Power', p. 331.

94. Levinas, 'Humanism and An-Archy', p. 48. Incidentally, in this passage Levinas anticipates the recent work of Roberto Esposito, who has argued that the 'general transition of humankind towards thingness' derives from the polarity between people's abstract existence as the subject of rights and their material, biological being (Esposito, *Third Person*, p. 94).

95. Foucault, *The Order of Things*, p. 422.
96. Levinas, *Totality and Infinity*, p. 281.
97. Ibid., p. 242.
98. Douzinas, *Human Rights and Empire*, p. 123.
99. Foucault, *The History of Sexuality Vol. 1*, p. 140.
100. Levinas, *Totality and Infinity*, p. 132.
101. This is a point emphasised in *Existence and Existents*, although at this stage Levinas had not developed the vocabulary of the dwelling that appears with particular lucidity in *Totality and Infinity*.

6

Law, Ethics and Political Subjectivity

This chapter begins with an outline of its central arguments as well as the concluding claims of the book as a whole. As covered in Chapter 4, applications of Levinas to law typically ask us to imagine law as a responsive site for the ethical encounter – whether in its institutions, its procedures, or reflected in its substance. This rests on a typically unstated but nevertheless unavoidable premise, that law operates as the servant of human will. This largely reflects how Levinas understood law himself, as being the necessary framework in which we do the hard work of creating social structures that do the best possible job of articulating the ethical bonds we have with each other. Law articulates being's essence, it is ontological, but it can be put to use in institutionalising a said for the sake of the other, as described by Levinas's passages on justice. But one should not lose sight of the assumptions we make if we entertain the idea that law can be easily instrumentalised as a product of wilful invention and a beneficent social apparatus. To assume that law is a mere tool at our disposal and the voice of justice is to ignore the vast bulk of critical writing about law ever since Marx, and to circumvent the injunction to understand the relation between law and ideology, power, language, the unconscious and the body. We can forgive such an omission in Levinas's work, but we should not afford ourselves the same indulgence. Accepting the idea that law is implicated within wider ideological apparatuses means understanding that law is not so much our invention, as we are the inventions of law.

Examining the relation between Levinas's philosophy, law, and the full range of critical approaches to law would require several further monographs. This book has adopted biopolitics – a set of ideas about which Levinas was often highly perceptive – as its critical framework, not least because it asks urgent questions of the qualified liberalism in Levinas's outlook, as well as the relationship between the juridical and the ontological.

The argument put forward in this respect has been that the general terrain of being, the fixity of which the subject seeks to 'escape' in the relation with the other, is affirmed and reified rather than put into question by law's operation. This is not to say that there is no internal coherence to the idea, say, of the ethically responsive judge, or of the human rights of the other. Notwithstanding some of the issues of technical detail, there is nothing intrinsically wrong as a whole with the legal form representing a vehicle for a Levinasian idea of justice. But rather, it is to say that for these ideas to become something other than utopian hopes there must first be the seismic changes necessary to substantially decouple law from the determination of life.

The task of linking Levinas's philosophy to a radical politics must address his position on Marxism and ideology. Reading Althusser, Levinas notes, consciousness is to be understood as a product of its 'objective or material conditions'.[1] Such an outlook entails the apparent risk that the emancipatory understanding of ourselves becomes dissolved into pure objectivity, forgetting the ethical provocation of the other. Whereas our ethical inclination might prompt us to attack the proletarianising function of ideology, he claims, ethics is quickly lost in the continuing trajectory of ideological critique that follows.[2] Yet for Levinas, the encounter with the other, 'like anti-ideology', has a rebellious potential for opening revolt, including where social injustice is 'balanced, governed by laws, subject to a power and constituting an order, a State, a city, a nation, a professional corporation'.[3] Levinas recognises here the radical potential of his work, which has elsewhere been drawn out more fully within an anarchic metapolitics described by Simon Critchley, and the liberation theory of Enrique Dussel.[4] Both see a profound political importance for Levinas in understanding the way that ethics can interrupt the hegemonic status quo.

This chapter, carrying with it some of the ideas about biopolitics from the previous chapter but also developing a more general set of claims about legal ontology, asks how we can conceive a way of thinking of Levinas and law that incorporates this sort of radicalism. An initial key premise necessary is the need to relinquish the temptation to regard law as a simple framework for justice, and also to relinquish the idea that ethics is a mere remedial supplement to the juridical edifice. As Emilios Christodoulidis has argued pointedly, critical thought fails when ethics is deployed merely to soften the operation of power to which it otherwise acquiesces.[5] Instead, this chapter focuses on the way that law and ontology determine each other and how ethics opens the human experience in their fissures. Levinas's occasional comments on the 'law of being', whilst almost certainly not intended to refer to law's juridical form, are revealed to be amongst his most prescient. The chapter ultimately seeks to delineate a Levinasian form of subjectivity defined specifically by its resistance to legal ontology. In doing so, it concludes that the pressing insight Levinas offers us on law is not how to make law ethical, but how ethics can teach us how to live despite and beyond the law.

Law, Nature and History

The temporality of modernity is characterised by its linearity and its continuity. In biopolitical practice, this temporality becomes rooted not only in the basic precepts of presence and coherence, but also in the very idea of history, such that law draws authority from and expresses a natural movement of materiality (Nazi biopolitics) or freedom (liberal biopolitics). We need to understand why law in particular is apt to express this experience of time. Chapter 3 has already explored the ways that law articulates a synchronic temporality, privileging the present/presence over the discontinuity of diachronous experience. Crucially, this is not merely identifiable in the content of law (to the extent that law comprises a continuous history of mutually supporting authorities) but also in legal reasoning, which can be understood as a phenomenological constitution of the legal present/presence in relation to past and future. Legal reasoning involves the flattening or synchronising of time through a function of the legal 'now.'

But to take this analysis further, it is also useful to examine Hannah Arendt's reflections on the temporality of law. There is little doubt that her analysis of totalitarianism describes and operates in the same analytic register as the works we now frame within the lexicon of biopolitics. She observes the departure from the idea of law codifying a set of moral or political 'oughts' to its governance via a normalised conception of what is, describing the way in which legitimacy refers back to a superficially incontestable conception of 'History or Nature'.[6] Rather than articulating 'standards of right and wrong', totalitarian governance applies these laws of nature/history 'directly to the "species", to mankind'.[7] Resonating with the debates on the deployment of legal strategies of exceptionalism, Arendt explains that this law is at the same time lawless, allowing for the suspension of positive laws and the arbitrary exercise of power by appealing to the higher laws that nature/history deliver. Arendt's repeated double reference to both nature and history is important. The normalised conception of life that is drawn upon must have the status of appearing natural, such that those who are applying power can 'claim to be neither just nor wise, but to know "scientifically"'.[8] Meanwhile, the temporality of totalitarian law appears on a linear and essential trajectory of history, in which society accelerates towards its logical fulfilment (in the Nazi regime, towards the purification of race).

Arendt notes, furthermore, the way in which temporality and change take on a new role in the relationship between law and subjectivity. Rather than law providing a stable framework in which the spontaneity and freedom of people can be exercised (representing the liberal ideal), one instead sees a reversal. As such, legally constituted spontaneity is erased through 'terror', and humans are fixated to a conception of their being that, conversely, allows for the movement of the laws of nature/history through their inevitable trajectory.[9]

Arendt claims that 'this movement, with its own beginning and its own end, can only be hindered by the new beginning and the individual end which the life of each man actually is'.[10] She therefore gestures towards an understanding of time which sees the subject seeking to transcend its own temporal fixity in being. For Levinas, this 'new beginning' would be experienced via the diachronic saying, in which the true freedom and potentiality for human creation is constituted in diastasis, in relation to time outside history, which is not my time but the 'time of the Other'.[11] Arendt therefore similarly understands that what threatens and what is sought to be suppressed by the laws of nature and history is the very creativity and potentiality of the human, its capacity to generate new conceptions of life that escape such laws.

Can Arendt's conception of law and time, which we can gradually link to that of Levinas, shed light on the liberal counterpart to totalitarian biopolitics? Kathrin Braun has noted that Arendt identified the same structure of temporality (which Braun denotes as 'processual' – that is, orientated towards fundamental underlying processes) in post-war Europe and particularly in the 'maintenance of the economic dynamic' of capitalist political economy.[12] As Braun notes, the specific terror that characterised Nazism is by no means essential to this temporality, which continues to operate 'to the extent that human activities are qualified and treated as mere means to feed an automatic, relentlessly proceeding paramount process'.[13] Totalitarianism, in Arendt's view, demands an acceleration of the laws of nature/history (contrasted with the fixity of the subjects captured within its conception of being). Meanwhile, within (neo-)liberal capitalism the rhetorical fetishisation of growth, development, and so on, expresses its own particular velocity of economic activity at the very foundation of the social, which, to follow the Marxist interpretation, law has the task of articulating. Yet we should also heed the infamous yet perceptive slogan that the dominance of capital and liberal democracy marks the 'end of history',[14] that this process finds its fulfilment in nothing other than itself. Such an 'end' does not mark the withdrawal of history, but its completion. In other words, a state of pure continuity. Such continuity finds expression in the ontologisation of otherness in the construction of life, in the fundamental *letting be* of humanity. Law understands human action as not meaningful for its own sake, but for the sake of being in general.

Whilst there are many of Levinas's reflections on the relation between temporality, ontology and subjectivity that could be useful in meditating on nature and history here, it is particularly helpful to consider the extended reflection in the chapter 'The Ethical Relation and Time' in *Totality and Infinity*. Insofar as the biopolitical conception of freedom relies upon factual matrices that determine the nature of human society, such 'freedom' must be distinctly ontological in Levinas's framework. Yet genuine freedom for him must come from 'outside totality', otherwise it becomes, at best, a form of mere 'indetermination within being' in which freedom effaces itself by becoming tied to the 'laws of a free being' that totality necessarily implies.[15] (Here we can pause to note the similar irony in the biopolitical operation of law in which one sees the destruction of freedom in the name of freedom.) The time of freedom is derived from the anticipation of a novel future that allows one not to be subsumed by the present, that is, 'to relate oneself to being as to a being to come, to maintain a distance with regard to being even while already coming under its grip'.[16] As Levinas makes absolutely explicit, the provocation of the other pierces and 'uproots' the subject from history.[17]

Yet how do we understand the following: 'Freedom is engraved on the stone of the tables on which laws are inscribed – it exists by virtue of this incrustation of an institutional existence'?[18] Levinas describes law as important to freedom, as it gives time – it protects the subject and provides a stable framework in which the subject can maintain its relation to being. This is without doubt true; in the lawlessness of pure chaos, in which the need simply to survive becomes primary, there can only be a dominance of the immediate present and an impossibility of taking up a meaningful relation with the future. But whilst providing what Levinas identifies as a condition of freedom, law also objectifies the subject in the universality of the order it institutes. There is 'tyranny' and an 'inhuman' quality to this order 'of the universal and of the impersonal'.[19] Law provides the solidity of a framework in which we can act and regulate our behaviour, yet it is at the same time a closure of the ethical in its translation into an objective framework.

It is worth reiterating that this idea of law in Levinas's work, caught between the attempted expression and the effective denial of the responsibility toward the other, is inadequate in itself and needs connection to a wider critique of power. But his ideas in *Totality and Infinity* are of particular interest here because they speak of the way in which the subject becomes objectified in the very institutions that purport to grant its freedom. This forms part of Levinas's analysis, later in the book, of the subject's accusative form, the way in which subjectivity emerges via the ethical challenge of the other. Constituted as a form of existential apology, the subject inevitably seeks redemption in the form of judgment. Apology is a particularly useful concept in this regard, denoting the trauma of subjectivity torn between its autonomy and its indebtedness to the other. To apologise is to take up a position, to speak and therefore to affirm oneself, yet at the same time to efface oneself, to take responsibility for one's presence. As a 'positive act', apology means taking up freedom and giving an account of one's freedom.[20] In this sense, Levinas appears to entertain both the common definition of apology as a form of repentance, but also its archaic Latin root (*apologia*), as a form of justification.

From where do we seek judgment of our apology? Here Levinas makes a distinction between politics and religion, categories that both require some degree of qualification.[21] One's political being concerns the manner in which the subject appears objectified in history. Here, judgment involves the application of universal laws and the assimilation of the subject and its singularity into totality. In effect, history negates apology, balancing debts and producing a continuity of presence in which subjects are reconciled into their being. It must be emphasised that this is a distinctly legal form of judgment. That is not to say it refers literally to the process of being on trial (although that would certainly be exemplary), but rather that it concerns the phenomenology of law as a whole, the manner in which the delicate human touch, the irremissible responsibility of sensuous human experience, in all its ecstasy and violence, becomes mediated through legal categories and concepts. What Levinas describes, on the other hand, as religious is to seek judgment beyond law, by appealing to the other.[22] It is only by going beyond law that apology can be maintained and responsibility affirmed without being discharged. Apology addresses the beyond of totality, in which the subject reclaims itself and resists its dissolution into (legal) ontology. Levinas explains that justice therefore requires going beyond justice, going 'behind the straight line of the law', due to being 'responsible beyond every limit fixed by an objective law'.[23]

It is this form of responsibility that Levinas describes as 'religious', in which one's singular relation with the infinitude of the other breaks the totality of one's embodiment within history. The points of connection between this analysis and the idea of the liberal state, explored in the previous chapter, should hopefully be relatively clear. Levinas identifies the structure of politics and law as necessary to effectuate the basic freedom we all need to realise ourselves initially, yet we have to recognise that liberalism is not 'all we need' to resist the tyranny of totality and to pursue the freedom we find in our constitutive relation with the other.

It is necessary to add to Levinas's analysis that the history expressed in the temporality of law is not authored by its subjects, but rather the other way around: we are authored by history. Again, biopolitics expresses this most forcefully, in the way we are produced as either normal, naturally entitled to our full expression as a matter of historical destiny, or as abnormal, denoting our irregularity or deviancy that can be disciplined or simply abandoned. Indeed, as biopolitical critique teaches, we are potentially suspended between this very distinction. When an objective and impersonal order of law comes into being, its effect is not simply to allow us to survive, to institute justice in the said, to grant the basic freedoms that express our responsibilities in objective terms. Rather, we must confront the idea that we are produced by law, which in turn serves historical conceptions of materiality and freedom. Eric Severson's authoritative work on Levinas and time notes his anxiety about the temporality of modernity, in which we each become, as Levinas put it, 'a mechanism among other mechanisms, small clocks reproducing the beating of astronomical time'.[24] Law serves to express precisely this temporal relation, in which the subject is enchained to scientistic determination of being in which the flowing of time is subordinated to the permanence of history.

This does not negate Levinas's insight for law. On the contrary, Levinas's injunction to go beyond the 'straight line' of the law prompts an understanding of ethics as rebellious. Resisting law becomes not merely the political expression of our ethical duties, but the very condition of finding our own subjectivity in this responsibility. The modalities of disruptive time that Levinas deploys – the diachronic nature of the saying, the infinite and messianic temporalities of the other – reveal the manner in which our experience of time is essential to this process. Ethics can provide a way out of the conceptions of humanity and history in which law enmeshes us. What follows in the next two sections is an attempt to trace, with Levinas, a middle path through the bipolar tendency of law in modernity, neither reducing the human to an accordance with the law of material being, nor reifying the human as an intangible expression of autonomous freedom.

Materiality's Law

It is notable that Slavoj Žižek, in an otherwise uncharitable appraisal of Levinas's ethics, would describe his philosophy as 'radically *antibiopolitical*' in the way in which it resists the practices of the management of life by addressing 'something *more* than life'.[25] This is no doubt true: Levinas's philosophy speaks of the provocation the subject feels to get out of the existence to which it is rooted, to escape. With the importance it places on the categories of the infinite and of times that are diachronically originary or futural, there is a crucial sense in which the Levinasian injunction appears to be to transcend the very lives that we lead. If, as the previous chapter has argued, we must confront the idea that law is, and increasingly so, not merely regulative of life, but productive and determinative of our conceptions of life, then we should explore the resources that he provides to understand our relation with such configurations, and specifically the scope for a politically resistant ethical relation.

In an interview in 1986, Levinas was asked how people can act unethically.[26] This is a pressing question, because the descriptive nature of Levinas's ethics might lead one to think that we are unconditionally ethical in all that we do. Such a position would entail that ethics is merely an interpretive term for understanding our existing behaviour. Of course, this is not the case – the fact that we are subject to a form of ethical command does not mean that we always comply (not to mention the irreducible ontological violence we always inflict due to the impossibility of fully discharging our duties). Levinas's response to this question is useful because he talks of the essential conflict between the struggle for life, the *conatus essendi*, and the ethical command. Our responsibility towards the other is what pulls us away from our commitment to securing our own lives, whilst the capacity to be absolutely unethical is given its justification precisely by this instinct to be primarily for-ourselves. When we act unethically it is because we prioritise ourselves above the other. That we can be drawn away from the *conatus essendi* is what characterises a form of life capable of ethics.

In developing his response to this issue further, Levinas talks of the way that ethics 'must be thought of outside the idea of force', and that ethics creates a 'rupture' in the 'law of being'. This law of being, Levinas goes on to explain, is also a 'law of evil'.[27] There is much to unpack here. The force that Levinas speaks of is a law of existence that flows from the *conatus essendi* itself. Associating it with evil is a striking way of describing what presents itself superficially as an elementary instinct of living, but Levinas clarifies further by introducing the case of Auschwitz. The connection here involves understanding Auschwitz as the logical end of a desire to protect, preserve and extend life. By illustrating his point in this way, Levinas makes clear – albeit implicitly – that he does not regard the 'law of being' as something merely personal, that inhabits each individual as a basic biological drive to persevere. Entrenching a concern to continue being by force, by law, is something that may find its fullest expression in the apparatus of sovereign power and the state. This allows us to supplement Levinas's analysis, to draw the necessary connection between the law of being, as the formation of structures of securing life by force, and the biopolitical form of governance in modernity. This is, incidentally, the same connection demanded by Agamben's claim that the camp is the 'nomos of the modern'.

If the idea of wanting to escape from life itself seems arresting at first, its full significance should be clear when we understand the capacity of ethics to disturb the logic of equivalence between life and law. Consider for a moment Esposito's interpretative framework, in which he identifies the paradigmatic expression of modern governance as 'immunitary', deploying its apparatuses to protect life even to the extent that it denigrates the very life in question.[28] Levinas, as if anticipating this homology of biological and regulative terms, talks of the way his own ethics posits a 'non-allergic' relation with the other.[29] Allergy is, of course, a form of immune response – more precisely an *auto*immune reaction in which the protective element extends to issue a harm to the host. By functioning to help the host continue to live, the allergy itself poses a threat to its wellbeing. This linkage helps us, first, to draw the crucial link between legal norm and biological and material structures, and second, to understand the profound danger where the legal expression of the continuity of life is not a containment of the material *within* law, but instead is their direct correspondence with each other. But more than this, he prompts us to see the significance of the human being defined by something more than materiality, or perhaps more fittingly, as an escape from one's materiality.

The reference to allergy continues a theme in Levinas's work that sees one's bodily form as something that rivets the subject, that allows us the experience of individual sovereignty yet at the same time is our encumbrance in the corporeal.[30] The phenomenologies of need, pleasure, nausea and shame offered in *On Escape* elucidate in perhaps the most visceral detail the way in which Levinas links the fixity of the biological with the need to get beyond being. To be trapped in the experience of nausea, the futile urge to undo oneself in the act of vomiting, in the shame of being enchained to oneself, is the very 'affirmation of Being'.[31] Furthermore, the 'need' that provokes the desire to escape in the first place is not posed as a lack of being, but as predicated on its 'plenitude'.[32] One further suggestion needs to be made though, which is whether all of this deserves the name 'life'. Is it true, as Žižek claimed, that what we want to transcend is life itself? Against the material rootedness of life, might we stay faithful to Levinas's humanism by claiming life in the ethical? In other words, what we seek to transcend is not life *per se*, but life reduced to the experience of totality. This would mean asking whether there is room to define life beyond its determination by the laws of being, and instead to take up Foucault's suggestion that '[i]t is not that life has been totally integrated into techniques that govern and administer it; it constantly escapes them'.[33]

Freedom's Law

If we are to pursue the line of thinking prompted by the confluence of law and the fixity of being, we might ask what becomes of our understanding of rights. Human rights, or what he tended to refer to as the 'rights of man', were written upon favourably by Levinas, as covered in Chapter 4. Can we maintain such faith in the compatibility between the essential structures of his thinking on the one hand, and rights reinterpreted through the critical lens posited in this chapter and the last, on the other?

It is not an original observation to say that human rights, quite manifestly, might as well not exist for hundreds of millions of people, including the people who need them the most. They provide a useful legal vocabulary for those privileged enough to seek legal redress for serious individual harm, or those lucky enough to have the privileged advocate on their behalf. But to assert their universal and unconditional possession has not prevented large portions of the human race from enduring the depravity of poverty, torture and death. We might recall that despite the utopian tone of his writing on the subject, Levinas spoke of the risk of rights within fully industrialised or totalitarian societies becoming denigrated by the very practices that they come to enable.[34] To the extent that political techniques hold the human as the central term of governance, their technologies may subordinate and enslave the element they were seeking to protect. Yet Levinas held faith, arguing that for as long as rights begin with the duty to uphold the rights of the other, rights will express the uniqueness of the subject against their dissolution into a general category of the human species and offer the promise of the subject's 'tearing loose from the determining order of nature'.[35]

The connection that needs to be made here, one which we cannot be sure Levinas would have intended, is that the determining order of nature from which rights extract us coincides intimately with his sage warnings of the subjection of mankind in the institution of rights. Having human rights means, necessarily, becoming accorded with a conception of the human. Here we can learn, again from Esposito, that being the subject of human rights in law deploys a duality in subjectivity, through which one is 'subjected to one's own objectification'[36] as a rights-holder. One must be tied to an abstract legal person, to an idea of being a legal entity, beyond one's bare materiality. One is therefore objectified precisely because one enjoys legal subjectivity in this context. Furthermore, Esposito directs his analysis towards Arendt's own reading of human rights' failure, not as a challenge of enforcement, but as woven into the very structure of rights themselves by virtue of this duality of the abstract and the material. As she argued in *The Origins of Totalitarianism*, the juridical form of human rights ensures that they never reach those who, due to the biopolitical instrumentalisation of this duality, have been reduced to their bare materiality.[37] In other words, the construction of humanity inherent in human rights is one that must expunge a purely material determination of particular categories of people. The biopolitical significance at play, of course, is that this distinction, built into the very logic of rights, allows for people to be subjected to their absolute dispossession. That inmates in Guantanamo have no rights, or that travellers in the UK can effectively have their rights suspended, is not incidental to but absolutely determined by the structure of rights. Incidentally, this explains why, conversely, it has become impossible for rights jurisprudence to be denied to purely abstract legal entities such as corporations, whose rights exist in a form that has no material counterpart whatsoever.

It is necessary to qualify that this critique is aimed at the juridical form of human rights, because this is distinct from certain aspects of the way Levinas understood the 'rights of the other', in particular the idea that we do not need to wait for such rights to be conferred before they can be asserted.[38] But it casts into light an important dynamic between human rights as they exist in law and human rights as they operate as *a priori* claims to the uniqueness and alterity of each individual. It is not simply the case that the former is inextricably bound to withdraw its protections from the people who need it most, but also that such people are most likely to have to deploy political force to assert the sort of radical right demanded by the latter.

This leaves rights in a particular quandary, whereby the most desperate demands for their assertion run counter to their very juridical form. This is not to say that the idea of rights must be dismissed. Jacques Rancière, disagreeing with Arendt's diagnosis, argues that because rights do not operate upon a rigid distinction between the norm and the exception, they provide the terms of political dissensus in which the disenfranchised voice themselves as subjects of the dignity that human rights promise.[39] The determination of what it means to be human should not be monopolised by the usual sites of biopolitical practice (including law), and is open to political contestation to those who live outside its parameters, a process by which bare life becomes politicised.[40] Rancière acknowledges that the politicised voice of those embodied as bare life 'could not be endorsed – it could not even be *heard* – by the lawmakers'.[41] But this caveat illuminates what is, for our purposes here, the crucial point, that the condition of the rights of the other, as the signification of the alterity of each person that wrests them from their ontological determination, is a resistance to the determinism of law. When Levinas talks of the uniqueness expressed by the 'rights of man', operating either despite or because of that person's 'subsumption under the category of the human species',[42] he alludes to the way that the idea of the human expressed in human rights is ontological. To voice the dignity of human uniqueness through the 'rights of man' means transcending and therefore challenging the very fixity of the idea of the human in law.

This argument can be extended to rights in general, which always in their juridical form posit the subject as a generic, abstract legal entity in accordance with a particular conception of our situatedness within a network of social relations. When I assert my rights in property I am secured to an articulation of being which has the distribution of private property – the intimate linkage between person and thing, and the market as a form of social ordering – as a defining characteristic. In the same way that human rights depend on a particular abstract idea of what it is to be human, a property right provides a legal existence to those who are capable of speaking through the accepted ontology, the said, of property. Essential to this is the exclusion of those who cannot express themselves through this language of property, not only those whose existence is one of dispossession (such as refugees or the homeless) but also those who accord with alternative ideas about what property means (such as travellers or squatters). To an extent, this is not saying anything about Levinas and law that should not already be clear by now. All expressions of the said do violence to the other. But rights allow us to understand with a little more precision how legal ontology pervades the determination of the subject. Law is not merely invoked to solve ethical dilemmas in the presence of the third. Law fundamentally informs our understanding of ourselves in the world. Every act that takes up the position of a property rights holder in relation to other such legal subjects – each turn of a key, closing of a door, each invitation, each route that we walk – is informed by an understanding of being that is supported by the legal apparatus of the state: it is legal ontology. Every time we speak and act through property relations we articulate and reinforce a particular Enlightenment idealist mode of being, predicated on the market-driven circulation of property amongst rationally-driven rights-bearing individuals, and by necessity we denigrate and exclude the living reality of those without property. There is, therefore, a form of emptiness to this legal ontology, in which people and their interrelations are formalised as generic legal subjects.

What ruptures this is the ethical experience, the shattering effect of the saying that opens my responsibility towards the other. I arrive home to find another person squatting on my land. The compulsion to assert my rights, to order them off my land and even to leave 'my' country, is shattered by the piercing alterity of their suffering, by the relation they assume with property that escapes my grasp. I am responsible. Crucially, the torsion in me is not merely the substitutive relation between same and other, but between law and law's other. I am the site in which law is called to account, and my responsibility for the other is assumed as a responsibility against the law. Levinas's claim that '[t]he better I accomplish my duty the fewer rights I have'[43] holds significance not merely in the sense of one's freedom being called into question by the other, and not merely in the way that the 'rights of the other' precede my own. The more I gesture to the other, the more I undo myself in hostage and substitution, the more that my subjectivity becomes a resistance to both my legal-ontological determination as a rights-holder and, therefore, to the edifice of the law itself.

Political Subjectivity

We are now in a position to recap some of the key arguments of this chapter and its predecessor, and to advance the concluding argument of the book. The idea that law emerges in the objectivity of a said that seeks to give effect to our most fundamental expressions of responsibility to each other is most persuasive in isolation from the critique of law's linkage with ideology and practices of power. Levinas himself conceived law as a procedure of justice in which ontology is produced as a thematisation of the same for the sake of the other. In other words, our conception of being is informed by the judgment provoked by the antecedent domain of ethics. What Levinas failed to appreciate are the myriad ways in which, on the contrary, law is a servant of our conception of being, the latter itself determined by considerably more insidious vectors of knowledge, power, capital, and so on. If we free ourselves from the project of trying to find a way of ethicising law, either recognising a compulsion to do justice to our ethical bindings in the balancing of legal adjudication or within the prescriptive content of legal norms, then we find Levinas's work to be replete with resources to think of ethics as a way of getting out of law. He gestures us towards thinking a space for the living of human life in our pre-ontological exposedness that is outside the form of life determined by the law's biopolitical trajectory. What Levinas gives is a way of under-standing life beyond law, one that, in being constituted in its critique of law, is inescapably political.

Of course, this does not mean life is isolated entirely from law. On a basic ontological level, this is not possible: as Levinas counsels, '[t]he entry of the third party is the very fact of consciousness',[44] meaning that the invocation of universally representable structures of being that find their expression in law is a basic and necessary component of social exist-ence. Insofar as the third is always present in a society of more than two people, and that it must be cognised with reference to structures of meaning that are objectively intelligible – insofar as 'it is impossible to escape the State'[45] – then law is an irreducible backdrop to life and an ever-present modality through which we understand ourselves. Yet the provocation that the other issues has the effect of constituting our respon-sibility and our freedom in the fissures and ruptures of law's ontological fabric. We must take seriously Levinas's lucidity in explaining that the ethical relation cannot be exhausted by law, that 'responsibility for the neighbour is precisely that which goes beyond legality'.[46] Ethics describes a signification and a relation in which the human encounter is other to law, and situates the experience of law's ontological violence in the most fundamental of intersubjective gestures.

This necessitates returning to the idea of anarchy in Levinas. As dis-cussed in Chapter 3, the other's proximity is anarchic because it operates without mediation through any principle or concept. It was also shown that in order to reconcile the centrality of anarchy to Levinas's thinking with a nuanced understanding of law, we might entertain the possibility of something that could be understood, paradoxically, as an 'anarchic law', where anarchy is anarchic for the sake of the law that forms in its wake.[47] Suggested here, instead, is that anarchy is anarchic for the sake of what it produces in the subject, a mode of what can be termed political subjectivity. This denotes a Levinasian subject that finds, in the proximal encounter with the other, a challenge to the fixity of the subject's understanding of itself in the world and, crucially, a challenge to the legal determination of the subject. What we know from Levinas is that the responsibility, hostage and substitution produced in this encounter *is* subjectivity itself, as the other in the same. What emerges, therefore, is a subject defined by, and indeed *as*, its own traumatic resistance against its being riveted to a conception of being articulated through legal structures. It is not that we critique the edifices of the law and the state, via the anarchic ethic challenge, as if they were exterior to us, as if we can somehow extricate ourselves and be positioned so as to adjudicate. The anarchic energy is a torsion between law and the other that takes place in, and *as*, the subject itself. It is the subjectivity of being against the law.

Simon Critchley, in arguing for Levinas to be read in the context of 'anarchic metapolitics' (somewhat differently to his suggestion for an anarchic law, considered in Chapter 3), is right to note the potentially radical implications of Levinas's idea of anarchy.[48] It is irreducible to a substantive political goal, effecting the disturbance of the political rather than setting down a positive programme of what to think or how to act. This is not, therefore, an argument for a determinate agenda of anarchism. As Levinas makes clear, his idea of anarchy operates prior to any distinction between freedom and unfreedom, or order and disorder. Characteristically, this reading of Levinas offers no comprehensive normative programme of political behaviour. Instead it offers a way in which, on a descriptive level, we can understand how people become motivated and impassioned, as agents for change.

As Victoria Tahmasebi-Birgani has rightly noted, Levinas can be found to offer occasional, fleeting gestures towards a radical politics that allows the process of ethical substitution to be read as 'a rebellion against injustice done to the other'.[49] Such a thinking recalls Enrique Dussel's understanding of Levinas's critical apparatus. For Dussel, Levinas resonates with Marx in elucidating the way in which hegemonic power excludes alterity, cutting through the ideological veil that allows such oppression to appear natural and neutral.[50] The responsibility taken by the subject for the excluded other, the way in which the other becomes the subject's unique concern, delivers a political imperative to criticise the ontological framework that excludes. For our purposes here, insofar as this framework is expressed through juridical structures, the ethically originated but profoundly political energy of the subject finds its voice in the critique of law.

If the central wager of the latter part of this book is correct, that we cannot count on law in late modernity to produce the same for the sake of the other, rather than for the sake of the same itself, then we are prompted to ask what happens to our conception of justice. Can we find another route to justice, one that does not rely on the law's ability to interrupt the synchrony and coherence of the ontology it voices? Instead, it might be more appropriate to consider how helpful the language of justice is in the first place. Levinas's philosophy might invite us to consider whether there is greater phenomenological significance to, on the contrary, the concept of injustice.[51] Justice is something never fully obtained in the Levinasian schema: it always fails, it is always marked by the very ontological violence that it seeks to remedy. Of course, this could require us to treat justice as a productive aporia, as a regulative horizon that demands that we continually undo and reconstitute the law, and its original violence, through acts of interpretation and judgment.[52] But the experience of injustice is primary, and not merely the absence of its opposite. The way in which the other's proximal signification calls my ontological understanding into question, making me accountable for myself as an expression of the inadequacy of the law's being, creates the trauma of injustice in me. I become accountable in my realisation that there is an other to the law, that law's violence is not merely found in its internal checks and balances, but in its very failure to represent the alterity of the human. The other's importance to me manifests in the way the other is absent from law, and in the way that my responsibility tears at me, demanding I uproot myself from the security that law provides me. What is produced in this encounter could be called political subjectivity, a subjectivity that is politicised by its unconditional ethical orientation into addressing the social and institutional structures that reflect and author legal ontology, energising and elucidating critique. A subjectivity constituted by the sense of injustice, caught between its determination in law and the affective touch of law's other.

Notes

1. Levinas, *Of God Who Comes to Mind*, p. 4.
2. Ibid.

3. Ibid., p. 9.
4. Despite his scepticism about the Marxist intellectual framework, one should note Levinas's proud approval of Latin American liberation theory in general, and specifically the writing of Enrique Dussel, which seeks to bring together Levinas's work with Marxist theory (Levinas, *Entre Nous*, p. 102).
5. Christodoulidis, 'Strategies of Rupture', p. 16.
6. Arendt, 'On the Nature of Totalitarianism', pp. 339–40.
7. Ibid., p. 340.
8. Ibid., p. 342.
9. Ibid.
10. Ibid.
11. See Levinas, *Otherwise than Being*, pp. 37–8. On 'the time of the Other', see Levinas, *Basic Philosophical Writings*, p. 50; and generally, Levinas, *Time and the Other*.
12. Braun, 'Biopolitics and Temporality', p. 17. In making this point, Braun is drawing upon Arendt's *On Violence*.
13. Braun, 'Biopolitics and Temporality', p. 17.
14. Fukuyama, 'The End of History'.
15. Levinas, *Totality and Infinity*, p. 225.
16. Ibid., p. 237.
17. Ibid., p. 52.
18. Ibid., p. 241.
19. Ibid., p. 242.
20. Ibid., p. 252.
21. Ibid., p. 253.
22. Levinas explains how 'before the neighbor I "compear" rather than appear' (Levinas, *Of God Who Comes to Mind*, p. 71). As Bettina Bergo's translator's note explains, 'compear' is a term used in French and Scots law, to denote one's presence in court. By compearing rather than appearing, Levinas stresses that it is the summons, the accusation of the other, and not the presence of self and other as if equals, that is crucial. One should also be careful to note that Levinas is talking figuratively and not of empirically juridical processes, having emphasised in the preceding paragraph that the ethical relation must go beyond the legal. Nevertheless, he invites some interesting comparisons between aspects of a figurative legal form of the other's accusation and the ontological realm of the juridical.
23. Levinas, *Totality and Infinity*, p. 245.
24. Severson is quoting a 1946 entry in the notebooks Levinas wrote

during wartime and shortly afterwards, which were published in 2009 (Levinas, *Carnet de Captivité et Autres Inédits*, p. 218). Quoted in Severson, *Levinas's Philosophy of Time*, p. 49.

25. Žižek, 'Neighbors and Other Monsters', pp. 149–50; original emphasis.
26. Levinas, 'Paradox of Morality', p. 175.
27. Ibid.
28. Esposito, *Bios*; Esposito, *Communitas*; Esposito, *Immunitas*.
29. Levinas, *Totality and Infinity*, p. 47.
30. Ibid., p. 164.
31. Levinas, *On Escape*, p. 68.
32. Ibid., p. 69.
33. Foucault, *The History of Sexuality Vol. I*, p. 143.
34. Levinas, *Outside the Subject*, p. 95.
35. Ibid., p. 92; see also p. 98.
36. Esposito, *Third Person*, p. 12.
37. Arendt, *The Origins of Totalitarianism*, pp. 299–300; See also Esposito, *Third Person*, pp. 68–9.
38. Levinas, *Outside the Subject*, p. 92.
39. Rancière, 'Who is the Subject of the Rights of Man?'.
40. Ibid., pp. 303–4; For an extended secondary discussion, see Schaap, 'Enacting the Right to Have Rights'.
41. Rancière, 'Who is the Subject of the Rights of Man?', p. 304.
42. Levinas, *Outside the Subject*, p. 92; See also on this particular aspect of Levinas's reflections on rights as a mechanism for expressing the uniqueness of alterity: Visker, 'The Inhuman Core of Human Dignity'.
43. Levinas, *Totality and Infinity*, p. 244.
44. Levinas, *Otherwise than Being*, pp. 157–8.
45. Levinas, *Difficult Freedom*, p. 178.
46. Levinas, *Of God Who Comes to Mind*, p. 71.
47. Critchley, 'Anarchic Law'.
48. Critchley, *Infinitely Demanding*, pp. 122–3. Critchley makes this observation with respect to the passages on anarchy in *Otherwise than Being*, particularly Levinas's explanation, reserved in the endnotes, that anarchy 'can only disturb the State – but in a radical way, making possible moments of negation *without any* affirmation' (Levinas, *Otherwise than Being*, p. 194). On the idea of anarchic metapolitics, see also Abensour, 'An-archy Between Metapolitics and Politics'.
49. Tahmasebi-Birgani, *Emmanuel Levinas and the Politics of Non-Violence*, p. 89.
50. Dussel, *Ethics of Liberation*, p. 217.

51. For further discussion of the primacy of injustice, see Stone, 'Levinas and Political Subjectivity'.
52. As reflected broadly in the arguments of Derrida, 'Force of Law'; See also de Ville, *Law as Absolute Hospitality*.

Bibliography

Abensour, Miguel, 'An-archy Between Metapolitics and Politics', *Parallax* 8 no. 3 (2002), pp. 5–18.

Acton, Thomas, (ed.), *Gypsy Politics and Traveller Identity* (Hatfield: University of Hertfordshire Press, 1997).

Agamben, Giorgio, *Homo Sacer: Sovereign Power and Bare Life* (Stanford: Stanford University Press, 1998).

Agamben, Giorgio, *Remnants of Auschwitz: The Witness and the Archive* (New York: Zone Books, 1999).

Alford, C. Fred, 'Levinas and Political Theory', *Political Theory* 32 no. 2 (2004), pp. 146–71.

Alford, C. Fred, 'Levinas and the Limits of Political Theory', in Marinos Diamantides (ed.), *Levinas, Law, Politics* (Oxford: Routledge-Cavendish, 2007), pp. 107–26.

Ali Khan, Liaquat, 'Temporality of Law', *McGeorge Law Review* 40 (2009), pp. 55–106.

Arendt, Hannah, 'On the Nature of Totalitarianism: An Essay in Understanding', in *Essays in Understanding 1930–1954. Formation, Exile, and Totalitarianism* (New York: Schocken Books, 1994), pp. 328–60.

Arendt, Hannah, *On Violence* (San Diego: Harcourt, 1970).

Arendt, Hannah, *The Origins of Totalitarianism* (New York: Harcourt, 1966).

Aston, Rhys, and Margaret Davies, 'Property in the World: On Collective Hosting and the "Ownership" of Communal Goods', *Law Text Culture* 17 (2013), pp. 211–39.

Atterton, Peter, 'Levinas's Skeptical Critique of Metaphysics and Anti-humanism', *Philosophy Today* 41 no. 4 (1997), pp. 491–506.

Baxi, Upendra, 'Judging Emmanuel Levinas? Some Reflections on

Reading *Levinas, Law, Politics*', *Modern Law Review* 72 no. 1 (2009), pp. 116–29.

Ben-Dor, Oren, *Thinking About Law in Silence with Heidegger* (Oxford: Hart, 2007).

Bergo, Bettina, *Levinas Between Ethics and Politics: For the Beauty that Adorns the Earth* (Dordrecht: Kluwer, 1999).

Braun, Kathrin, 'Biopolitics and Temporality in Arendt and Foucault', *Time and Society* 16 no. 1 (2007), pp. 5–23.

Brooks, Peter, and Paul Gewirtz (eds), *Law's Stories: Narrative and Rhetoric in the Law* (New Haven: Yale University Press, 1996).

Brown, Philip, and Pat Niner, *Assessing Local Authorities' Progress in Meeting the Accommodation Needs of Gypsy and Traveller Communities in England* (Manchester: Equality and Human Rights Commission, 2009).

Burggraeve, Roger, 'The Good and Its Shadow: The View of Levinas on Human Rights as the Surpassing of Political Rationality', *Human Rights Review* 6 no. 2 (2005), pp. 80–101.

Burggraeve, Roger, *The Wisdom of Love in the Service of Love: Emmanuel Levinas on Justice, Peace and Human Rights* (Milwaukee: Marquette University Press, 2002).

Butler, Judith, *Precarious Life: The Powers of Mourning and Violence* (London: Verso, 2004).

Cadava, Eduardo, Peter Connor and Jean-Luc Nancy (eds), *Who Comes After the Subject?* (London: Routledge, 1991).

Calarco, Matthew, 'Deconstruction is Not Vegetarianism: Humanism, Subjectivity, and Animal Ethics', *Continental Philosophy Review* 37 (2004), pp. 175–201.

Calarco, Matthew, 'Faced by Animals', in Peter Atterton and Matthew Calarco (eds), *Radicalizing Levinas* (Albany: SUNY Press, 2010), pp. 113–33.

Caygill, Howard, *Levinas and the Political* (London: Routledge, 2002).

Cemlyn, Sarah, Margaret Greenfields, Sally Burnett, Zoe Matthews and Chris Whitwell, *Inequalities Experienced by Gypsy and Traveller Communities: A Review* (Manchester: Equality and Human Rights Commission, 2009).

Christodoulidis, Emilios, 'Strategies of Rupture', *Law and Critique* 20 no. 1 (2009), pp. 3–26.

Ciaramelli, Fabio, 'Comparison of Incomparables', *Parallax* 8 no. 3 (2002), pp. 45–58.

Clifton-Soderstrom, Michelle, 'Levinas and the Patient as Other:

The Ethical Foundation of Medicine', *The Journal of Medicine and Philosophy* 28 no. 4 (2003), pp. 447–60.

Committee of Public Safety, '"My Place in the Sun": Reflections on the Thought of Emmanuel Levinas', *Diacritics* 26 no. 1 (1996), pp. 3–10.

Conklin, William, 'The Invisible Author of Legal Authority', *Law and Critique* 7 no. 2 (1996), pp. 173–92.

Conklin, William, *The Phenomenology of Modern Legal Discourse: The Juridical Production and the Disclosure of Suffering* (Aldershot: Ashgate, 1998).

Conklin, William, 'The Trace of Legal Idealism in Derrida's Grammatology', *Philosophy and Social Criticism* 22 no. 5 (1996), pp. 17–42.

Conklin, William, 'The Trap', *Law and Critique* 13 no. 1 (2002), pp. 1–29.

Cooper, Davina, 'Opening Up Ownership: Community Belonging, Belongings, and the Productive Life of Property', *Law and Social Inquiry* 32 no. 3 (2007), pp. 625–64.

Cornell, Drucilla, *The Philosophy of the Limit* (London: Routledge, 1992).

Cornell, Drucilla, 'Post-Structuralism, the Ethical Relation, and the Law', *Cardozo Law Review* 9 (1988), pp. 1591–628.

Cornell, Drucilla, Michael Rosenfeld and David Gray Carlson (eds), *Deconstruction and the Possibility of Justice* (London: Routledge, 1992).

'The Counted: People Killed by Police in the US', *The Guardian*, *http://www.theguardian.com/us-news/ng-interactive/2015/jun/01/the-counted-police-killings-us-database* (last accessed 1 September 2015).

Critchley, Simon, 'Anarchic Law', in Desmond Manderson (ed.), *Essays on Levinas and Law: A Mosaic* (Basingstoke: Palgrave Macmillan, 2009), pp. 203–11.

Critchley, Simon, *Ethics, Politics, Subjectivity: Essays on Derrida, Levinas, and Contemporary French Thought* (London: Verso, 1999).

Critchley, Simon, 'Five Problems in Levinas's View of Politics and the Sketch of a Solution to Them', *Political Theory* 32 no. 2 (2004), pp. 172–85.

Critchley, Simon, *Infinitely Demanding: Ethics of Commitment, Politics of Resistance* (London: Verso, 2007).

Critchley, Simon, 'Prolegomena to Any Post-Deconstructive Subjectivity', in Simon Critchley and Peter Dews (eds), *Deconstructive Subjectivities* (Albany: State University of New York Press, 1996), pp. 13–45.

Crowe, Jonathan, 'Levinasian Ethics and Animal Rights', *Windsor Yearbook of Access to Justice* 27 (2008), pp. 313–28.

Crowe, Jonathan, 'Levinasian Ethics and Legal Obligation', *Ratio Juris* 19 no. 4 (2006), pp. 421–33.

Crowe, Jonathan, 'Levinasian Ethics and the Concept of Law', in Desmond Manderson (ed.), *Essays on Levinas and Law: A Mosaic* (Basingstoke: Palgrave Macmillan, 2009), pp. 39–54.

Davidson, Scott, 'The Rights of the Other: Levinas and Human Rights', in Scott Davidson and Diane Perpich (eds), *Totality and Infinity at 50* (Pittsburgh: Duquesne University Press, 2011), pp. 171–87.

Davies, Margaret, 'Queer Property, Queer Persons: Self-Ownership and Beyond', *Social and Legal Studies* 8 no. 3 (1999), pp. 327–52.

Davis, Colin, 'Levinas at 100', *Paragraph* 29 no. 3 (2006), pp. 95–104.

de Villes, Jacques, *Jacques Derrida: Law as Absolute Hospitality* (Abingdon: Routledge, 2011).

de Villes, Jacques, 'Rethinking the Notion of a "Higher Law": Heidegger and Derrida on the Anaximander Fragment', *Law and Critique* 20 no. 1 (2009), pp. 59–78.

Derrida, Jacques, *Adieu to Emmanuel Levinas* (Stanford: Stanford University Press, 1999).

Derrida, Jacques, 'Force of Law: "The Mystical Foundation of Authority"', *Cardozo Law Review* 11 (1990), pp. 919–1045.

Derrida, Jacques, *The Gift of Death and Literature in Secret* (London: University of Chicago Press, 1995).

Derrida, Jacques, *Limited Inc*. (Evanston: Northwestern University Press, 1998).

Derrida, Jacques, *Of Grammatology* (Baltimore: Johns Hopkins University Press, 1998).

Derrida, Jacques, *Of Hospitality* (Stanford: Stanford University Press, 2000).

Derrida, Jacques, *The Politics of Friendship* (London: Verso, 2005).

Derrida, Jacques, 'Violence and Metaphysics: An Essay on the Thought of Emmanuel Levinas', in Jacques Derrida, *Writing and Difference* (London: Routledge, 2001), pp. 97–192.

Derrida, Jacques, and Pierre-Jean Labarriere, *Altérités* (Paris: Editions Osiris, 1986).

Devlin, Lord Patrick, *The Enforcement of Morals* (Oxford: Oxford University Press, 1965).

Diamantides, Marinos, *The Ethics of Suffering: Modern Law, Philosophy and Medicine* (Aldershot: Ashgate, 2000).

Diamantides, Marinos, 'From Escape to Hostage', in Asher Horowitz and Gad Horowitz (eds), *Difficult Justice: Commentaries on*

Levinas and Politics (Toronto: University of Toronto Press, 2006), pp. 191–220.

Diamantides, Marinos, 'Levinas and Critical Legal Thought: Imbroglio, Opera Buffa, Divine Comedy?', in Marinos Diamantides (ed.), *Levinas, Law, Politics* (Oxford: Routledge-Cavendish, 2007), pp. 179–215.

Diamantides, Marinos, (ed.), *Levinas, Law, Politics* (Oxford: Routledge-Cavendish, 2007).

Douzinas, Costas, *The End of Human Rights* (Oxford: Hart, 2000).

Douzinas, Costas, *Human Rights and Empire: The Political Philosophy of Cosmopolitanism* (Oxford: Hart, 2005).

Douzinas, Costas, 'Theses on Law, History and Time', *Melbourne Journal of International Law* 7 (2006), pp. 13–27.

Douzinas, Costas, and Ronnie Warrington, '"A Well-Founded Fear of Justice": Law and Ethics in Postmodernity', *Law and Critique* 2 no. 2 (1991), pp. 115–47.

Douzinas, Costas, and Ronnie Warrington, 'The Face of Justice: A Jurisprudence of Alterity', *Social and Legal Studies* 3 no. 3 (1994), pp. 405–25.

Douzinas, Costas, and Ronnie Warrington, *Justice Miscarried: Ethics and Aesthetics in Law* (London: Harvester Wheatsheaf, 1994).

Douzinas, Costas, and Ronnie Warrington with Shaun McVeigh, *Postmodern Jurisprudence: The Law of Text in the Texts of Law* (London: Routledge, 1991).

Dussel, Enrique, *Ethics of Liberation in the Age of Globalization and Exclusion* (London: Duke University Press, 2013).

Dworkin, Ronald, 'A Reply by Ronald Dworkin', in Marshall Cohen (ed.), *Ronald Dworkin and Contemporary Jurisprudence* (London: Duckworth, 1984), pp. 247–300.

Dworkin, Ronald, *Justice in Robes* (Cambridge, MA: Belknap Press, 2006).

Dworkin, Ronald, *Law's Empire* (Oxford: Hart, 2003).

Dworkin, Ronald, *Taking Rights Seriously* (London: Bloomsbury Academic, 1977).

Dworkin, Ronald, 'What Liberalism Isn't', *New York Review of Books*, 20 January 1983, pp. 47–50.

Esposito, Roberto, *Bios: Biopolitics and Philosophy* (London: University of Minnesota Press, 2008).

Esposito, Roberto, *Communitas: The Origin and Destination of Community* (Stanford: Stanford University Press, 2010).

Esposito, Roberto, *Immunitas: The Protection and Negation of Life* (Cambridge: Polity, 2011).

Esposito, Roberto, *Third Person: Politics of Life and Philosophy of the Impersonal* (Cambridge: Polity, 2012).

Ewald, François, 'Norms, Discipline, and the Law', *Representations* 30 (1990), pp. 138–61.

Ferreira da Silva, Denise, 'No Bodies: Law, Raciality and Violence', *Griffith Law Review* 18 (2009), pp. 212–36.

Fish, Stanley, *Doing What Comes Naturally: Change, Rhetoric and the Practice of Theory in Literary and Legal Studies* (Oxford: Clarendon, 1989).

Fisk, Milton, 'History and Reason in Rawls' Moral Theory', in Norman Daniels (ed.), *Reading Rawls: Critical Studies on Rawls' A Theory of Justice* (Stanford: Stanford University Press, 1989), pp. 53–80.

Fitzpatrick, Peter, 'The Abstracts and Brief Chronicles of the Time: Supplementing Jurisprudence', in Peter Fitzpatrick (ed.), *Dangerous Supplements: Resistance and Renewal in Jurisprudence* (London: Pluto Press, 1991), pp. 1–33.

Fitzpatrick, Peter, (ed.), *Dangerous Supplements: Resistance and Renewal in Jurisprudence* (London: Pluto Press, 1991).

Fitzpatrick, Peter, *Modernism and the Grounds of Law* (Cambridge: Cambridge University Press, 2001).

Flyvbjerg, Bent, 'Planning and Foucault: In Search of the Dark Side of Planning Theory', in Philip Allmendinger and Mark Tewdwr-Jones (eds), *Planning Futures: New Directions for Planning Theory* (London: Routledge, 2002), pp. 44–62.

Foucault, Michel, *The History of Sexuality Vol. 1* (London: Penguin, 1998).

Foucault, Michel, *The Order of Things: An Archaeology of the Human Sciences* (London: Routledge, 2002).

Foucault, Michel, 'The Politics of Health in the Eighteenth Century', in Michel Foucault, *Power: The Essential Works of Foucault 1954–1984*, ed. James D. Faubion (London: Penguin, 2002), pp. 90–105.

Foucault, Michel, *Security, Territory, Population: Lectures at the Collège de France 1977–1978* (Basingstoke: Palgrave Macmillan, 2009).

Foucault, Michel, *Society Must Be Defended: Lectures at the Collège de France 1975–76* (London: Penguin, 2003).

Foucault, Michel, 'The Subject and Power', in Michel Foucault, *Power: The Essential Works of Foucault 1954–1984*, ed. James D. Faubion (London: Penguin, 2002), pp. 326–48.

Fraser, Angus, *The Gypsies* (Oxford: Blackwell, 1992).

French, Rebecca R., 'Time in the Law', *University of Colorado Law Review* 72 (2001), pp. 663–748.

Fukuyama, Francis, 'The End of History', *The National Interest* (Summer 1989), pp. 3–18.

Gauthier, David J., *Martin Heidegger, Emmanuel Levinas and the Politics of Dwelling* (Plymouth: Lexington Books, 2011).

Gibbs, Robert, *Correlations in Rosenzweig and Levinas* (Princeton: Princeton University Press, 1992).

Gibbs, Robert, 'Law and Ethics', *Revista Portuguesa de Filosofia* 62 (2006), pp. 395–407.

Golder, Ben, 'The Distribution of Death: Notes Towards a Bio-political Theory of Criminal Law', in Matthew Stone, Illan rua Wall and Costas Douzinas (eds), *New Critical Legal Thinking: Law and the Political* (Abingdon: Routledge, 2012), pp. 91–111.

Golder, Ben, and Peter Fitzpatrick, *Foucault's Law* (Abingdon: Routledge, 2009).

Gordon, Neve, 'Foucault's Subject: An Ontological Reading', *Polity* 31 no. 3 (1999), pp. 395–414.

Goyal, Reena, 'Serving Justice Through Authority: A Phenomenological Approach to the Authority of Law', *University of Toronto Faculty of Law Review* 62 no. 1 (2004), pp. 29–60.

Greenhouse, Carol J., 'Just in Time: Temporality and the Cultural Legitimation of Law', *Yale Law Journal* 98 (1989), pp. 1631–51.

Hart, H. L. A., 'Are There Any Natural Rights', *The Philosophical Review* 64 no. 2 (1955), pp. 175–91.

Hart, H. L. A., *The Concept of Law* (Oxford: Oxford University Press, 2012).

Hart, H. L. A., *Law, Liberty and Morality* (London: Oxford University Press, 1963).

Hawes, Derek, and Barbara Perez, *The Gypsy and the State: The Ethnic Cleansing of British Society*, 2nd edn (Bristol: Policy Press, 1996).

Heidegger, Martin, *Basic Writings* (London: Routledge, 1993).

Heidegger, Martin, *Being and Time* (Oxford: Blackwell, 1962).

Herzog, Annabel, 'Is Liberalism "All We Need"? Levinas's Politics of Surplus', *Political Theory* 30 no. 2 (2002), pp. 204–27.

Hunt, Alan, and Gary Wickham, *Foucault and Law* (London: Pluto Press, 1994).

Husserl, Edmund, *Cartesian Meditations: An Introduction to Phenomenology* (London: Kluwer, 1999).

Husserl, Edmund, *Logical Investigations Volume 1* (Abingdon: Routledge, 2001).

Jameson, Frederic, *The Seeds of Time* (New York: Columbia University Press, 1994).

Jones, Tim, Marc Willers, and Angus Murdoch, 'Planning Law', in Chris Johnson and Marc Willers (eds), *Gypsy and Traveller Law*, 2nd edn (London: LAG, 2007), pp. 69–112.

Keenan, Sarah, *Subversive Property: Law and the Production of Spaces of Belonging* (Abingdon: Routledge, 2014).

Kelsen, Hans, *Pure Theory of Law* (Berkeley: University of California Press, 1967).

Lacan, Jacques, *The Seminar of Jacques Lacan: The Psychoses 1955–1956* (New York: W. W. Norton, 1993).

Lemke, Thomas, 'An Indigestible Meal? Foucault, Governmentality and State Theory', *Distinktion: Scandinavian Journal of Social Theory* 8 no. 2 (2007), pp. 43–64.

Lemke, Thomas, 'The Risks of Security: Liberalism, Biopolitics, and Fear', in Vanessa Lemm and Miguel Vatter (eds), *The Government of Life: Foucault, Biopolitics, and Neoliberalism* (New York: Fordham University Press, 2014), pp. 59–74.

Lemm, Vanessa, and Miguel Vatter (eds), *The Government of Life: Foucault, Biopolitics, and Neoliberalism* (New York: Fordham University Press, 2014).

Leung, Gilbert, and Matthew Stone, 'Otherwise than Hospitality: A Disputation on the Relation of Ethics to Law and Politics', *Law and Critique* 20 no. 2 (2009), pp. 193–206.

Levinas, Emmanuel, *Alterity and Transcendence* (London: Athlone, 1999).

Levinas, Emmanuel, *Basic Philosophical Writings* (Bloomington and Indianapolis: Indiana University Press, 1996).

Levinas, Emmanuel, *Beyond the Verse: Talmudic Readings and Lectures* (London: Continuum, 2007).

Levinas, Emmanuel, *Carnet de Captivité et Autres Inédits*, ed. Rodolphe Calin and Catherine Chalier (Paris: Grasset/Imec, 2009).

Levinas, Emmanuel, *Difficult Freedom: Essays on Judaism* (Baltimore: Johns Hopkins University Press, 1990).

Levinas, Emmanuel, *Entre Nous: Thinking-of-the-Other* (London: Continuum, 2006).

Levinas, Emmanuel, 'Ethics and Politics', in Sean Hand (ed.), *The Levinas Reader* (Oxford: Blackwell, 1989), pp. 289–97.

Levinas, Emmanuel, *Existence and Existents* (Pittsburgh: Duquesne University Press, 2001).

Levinas, Emmanuel, *God, Death and Time* (Stanford: Stanford University Press, 2001).

Levinas, Emmanuel, 'Humanism and An-archy', in Emmanuel Levinas, *Humanism of the Other* (Urbana and Chicago: University of Illinois Press, 2003), pp. 45–57.

Levinas, Emmanuel, *Les Imprevus de L'Histoire* (Montpellier: Fata Morgana, 1994).

Levinas, Emmanuel, *In the Time of the Nations* (London: Continuum, 2007).

Levinas, Emmanuel, *Is it Righteous to Be?* (Stanford: Stanford University Press, 2001).

Levinas, Emmanuel, 'Martin Heidegger and Ontology', *Diacritics* 26 no. 1 (1996), pp. 11–32.

Levinas, Emmanuel, *Of God Who Comes to Mind* (Stanford: Stanford University Press, 1998).

Levinas, Emmanuel, *On Escape* (Stanford: Stanford University Press, 2003).

Levinas, Emmanuel, *Otherwise Than Being or Beyond Essence* (Pittsburgh: Duquesne University Press, 1998).

Levinas, Emmanuel, *Outside the Subject* (London, Continuum, 2008).

Levinas, Emmanuel, 'The Paradox of Morality: An Interview with Emmanuel Levinas', in Robert Bernasconi and David Wood (eds), *The Provocation of Levinas: Rethinking the Other* (London: Routledge, 1988), pp. 168–80.

Levinas, Emmanuel, 'Philosophy and Awakening', in Eduardo Cadava, Peter Connor and Jean-Luc Nancy (eds), *Who Comes After the Subject?* (London: Routledge, 1991), pp. 206–16.

Levinas, Emmanuel, 'Reflections on the Philosophy of Hitlerism', *Critical Inquiry* 17 (1990), pp. 63–71.

Levinas, Emmanuel, *The Theory of Intuition in Husserl's Phenomenology* (Evanston: Northwestern University Press, 1995).

Levinas, Emmanuel, *Time and the Other* (Pittsburgh: Duquesne University Press, 1987).

Levinas, Emmanuel, *Totality and Infinity: An Essay on Exteriority* (Pittsburgh: Duquesne University Press, 1969).

Loughnan, Claire, 'Detention and Dwelling: Levinas and the Refuge of the Asylum Seeker', *Law, Text, Culture* 11 (2007), pp. 252–71.

MacIntyre, Alasdair, *Dependent Rational Animals: Why Human Beings Need the Virtues* (London: Bloomsbury Academic, 2013).

Macpherson, C. B., *The Political Theory of Possessive Individualism: Hobbes to Locke* (Oxford: Oxford University Press, 1962).

Malka, Salomon, *Emmanuel Levinas: His Life and Legacy* (Pittsburgh: Duquesne University Press, 2006).

Manderson, Desmond, 'Emmanuel Levinas and the Philosophy of Negligence', *Tort Law Review* 14 (2006), pp. 1–18.

Manderson, Desmond, (ed.), *Essays on Levinas and Law: A Mosaic* (Basingstoke: Palgrave Macmillan, 2009).

Manderson, Desmond, 'Here I Am: Illuminating and Delimiting Responsibility', in Marinos Diamantides (ed.), *Levinas, Law, Politics* (Oxford: Routledge-Cavendish, 2007), pp. 145–64.

Manderson, Desmond, *Proximity, Levinas and the Soul of Law* (London: McGill-Queens University Press, 2006).

McDaniel, Robb A., 'Garden-Variety Liberals: Discovering Eden in Levinas and Locke', *Polity* 34 no. 2 (2001), pp. 117–39.

McLeod, Ian, *Legal Theory*, 6th edn (Basingstoke: Palgrave Macmillan, 2012).

Metselaar, Suzanne, 'When Neighbours Become Numbers: Levinas and the Inhospitality of Dutch Asylum Policy', *Parallax* 11 no. 1 (2005), pp. 61–9.

Mouffe, Chantal, *On the Political* (London: Routledge, 2005).

Nancy, Jean-Luc, and Philippe Lacoue-Labarthe, *Retreating the Political* (London: Routledge, 1997).

Niner, Pat, *Local Authority Gypsy/Traveller Sites in England* (London: Office of the Deputy Prime Minister, 2003).

Nortvedt, Per, 'Levinas, Justice and Healthcare', *Medicine, Health Care and Philosophy* 6 no. 1 (2003), pp. 25–34.

Nussbaum, Martha, *Frontiers of Justice: Disability, Nationality, Species Membership* (London: Harvard University Press, 2006).

Okely, Judith, *The Traveller-Gypsies* (Cambridge: Cambridge University Press, 1983).

Penner, James, *The Idea of Property in Law* (Oxford: Clarendon, 1997).

Peperzak, Adriaan, *Beyond: The Philosophy of Emmanuel Levinas* (Evanston: Northwestern University Press, 1997).

Peperzak, Adriaan, *To the Other: An Introduction to the Philosophy of Emmanuel Levinas* (West Lafayette: Purdue University Press, 1993).

Perpich, Diane, *The Ethics of Emmanuel Levinas* (Stanford: Stanford University Press, 2008).

Perpich, Diane, 'Getting Down to Cases: Can a Levinasian Ethics Generate Norms?', in Desmond Manderson (ed.), *Essays on Levinas and Law: A Mosaic* (Basingstoke: Palgrave Macmillan, 1999), pp. 21–38.

Ploger, John, 'Foucault's Dispositif and the City', *Planning Theory* 7 no. 1 (2008), pp. 51–70.

Pogany, Istvan, *The Roma Café: Human Rights and the Plight of the Romani People* (London: Pluto, 2004).

Poirié, François, *Emmanuel Lévinas: Qui Êtes-Vous?* (Lyon: Editions la Manufacture, 1987).

Pugliese, Joseph, 'The Reckoning of Possibles: Asylum Seekers, Justice and the Indigenisation of the Levinasian Third', *Australian Feminist Law Journal* 34 (2011), pp. 23–42.

Pugliese, Joseph, *State Violence and the Exception of Law: Biopolitical Caesurae of Torture, Black Sites, Drones* (Abingdon: Routledge, 2013).

Radin, Margaret, 'Market-Inalienability', *Harvard Law Review* 100 no. 8 (1987), pp. 1847–937.

Radin, Margaret, 'Property and Personhood', *Stanford Law Review* 34 (1982), pp. 957–1015.

Rancière, Jacques, 'Who is the Subject of the Rights of Man?', *South Atlantic Quarterly* 103 no. 2/3 (2004), pp. 297–310.

Rastogi, Sonya, Tallese D. Johnson, Elizabeth M. Hoeffel, and Malcolm P. Drewery, Jr., 'The Black Population: 2010', *United States Census Bureau*, September 2011, available at *http://www.census.gov/prod/cen2010/briefs/c2010br-06.pdf* (last accessed 6 January 2016).

Rawls, John, *Political Liberalism* (New York: Columbia University Press, 2005).

Rawls, John, *A Theory of Justice* (Cambridge, MA: Belknap Press, 2005).

Ricoeur, Paul, 'Otherwise: A Reading of Emmanuel Levinas's *Otherwise than Being or Beyond Essence*', *Yale French Studies* 104 (2004), pp. 82–99.

Rolland, Jacques, 'Getting Out of Being by a New Path', in Emmanuel Levinas, *On Escape* (Stanford: Stanford University Press, 2003), pp. 3–48.

Rose, Gillian, *The Broken Middle: Out of Our Ancient Society* (Oxford: Blackwell, 1992).

Rose, Gillian, *Mourning Becomes the Law: Philosophy and Representation* (Cambridge: Cambridge University Press, 1996).

Sandland, Ralph, 'Developing a Jurisprudence of Difference: The Protection of the Human Rights of Travelling Peoples by the European Court of Human Rights', *Human Rights Law Review* 8 no. 3 (2008), pp. 475–516.

Schaap, Andrew, 'Enacting the Right to Have Rights: Jacques Rancière's Critique of Hannah Arendt', *European Journal of Political Theory* 10 no. 1 (2011), pp. 22–45.

Schmitt, Carl, *The Concept of the Political* (New Brunswick: Rutgers University Press, 1976).

Sederberg, Carl, 'Resaying the Human: Levinas Beyond Humanism and Antihumanism' (doctoral thesis, Södertörn University, 2010).

Simmons, William, *An-Archy and Justice: An Introduction to Emmanuel Levinas' Political Thought* (Oxford: Lexington, 2003).

Simmons, William, *Human Rights Law and the Marginalized Other* (Cambridge: Cambridge University Press, 2011).

Simmons, William, 'The Third: Levinas's Theoretical Move from Anarchical Ethics to the Realm of Justice and Politics', *Philosophy and Social Criticism* 25 no. 6 (1999), pp. 83–104.

Simons, Jon, *Foucault and the Political* (London: Routledge, 1995).

Sparrow, Tom, *Levinas Unhinged* (Arlesford: Zero Books, 2013).

Stewart, Michael, 'The Puzzle of Roma Persistence: Group Identity Without a Nation', in Thomas Acton (ed.), *Gypsy Politics and Traveller Identity* (Hatfield: University of Hertfordshire Press, 1997), pp. 82–96.

Stewart, Michael, *The Time of the Gypsies* (Oxford: Westview Press, 1997).

Stone, Ira, *Reading Levinas/Reading Talmud: An Introduction* (Philadelphia: The Jewish Publication Society, 1998).

Stone, Matthew, 'Biopolitics and Movement: A History of Travellers and the Law', *Liverpool Law Review* 32 no. 1 (2011), pp. 49–63.

Stone, Matthew, 'Law, Ethics and Levinas's Concept of Anarchy', *Australian Feminist Law Journal* 35 (2011), pp. 89–105.

Stone, Matthew, 'Levinas and Political Subjectivity in an Age of Global Biopower', *Law, Culture and the Humanities* 6 no. 1 (2010), pp. 105–23.

Stone, Matthew, 'Life Beyond Law: Questioning a Return to Origins', in Matthew Stone, Illan rua Wall and Costas Douzinas (eds), *New Critical Legal Thinking: Law and the Political* (Abingdon: Routledge, 2012), pp. 198–211.

Stone, Matthew, Illan rua Wall and Costas Douzinas (eds), *New Critical Legal Thinking: Law and the Political* (Abingdon: Routledge, 2012).

Strasser, Stephan, *Jenseits von Sein und Zeit: Eine Einführung in Emmanuel Levinas Philosophie* (The Hague: Martinus Nijhoff, 1978).

Stychin, Carl, 'Unmanly Diversions: The Construction of the Homosexual Body (Politic) in English Law', *Osgoode Hall Law Journal* 32 no. 3 (1994), pp. 503–36.

Tahmasebi-Birgani, Victoria, 'Does Levinas Justify or Transcend

Liberalism? Levinas on Human Liberation', *Philosophy and Social Criticism* 36 no. 5 (2010), pp. 523–44.

Tahmasebi-Birgani, Victoria, *Emmanuel Levinas and the Politics of Non-Violence* (London: University of Toronto Press, 2014).

Tamanaha, Brian, 'Conceptual Analysis, Continental Social Theory, and CLS', *Rutgers Law Journal* 32 (2009), pp. 281–306.

Taylor, Mark C., *Altarity* (Chicago: Chicago University Press, 1987).

Tiemersma, Douwe, 'Ontology and Ethics in the Foundation of Medicine and the Relevance of Levinas' View', *Theoretical Medicine* 8 no. 2 (1987), pp. 127–33.

Topolski, Anya, '*Relationality* as a "Foundation" for Human Rights: Exploring the Paradox with Hannah Arendt and Emmanuel Levinas', *Theoria and Praxis* 2 no. 1 (2014), pp. 1–17.

Valverde, Mariana, 'Law Versus History: Foucault's Genealogy of Modern Sovereignty', in Michael Dillon and Andrew W. Neal (eds), *Foucault on Politics, Security and War* (Basingstoke: Palgrave Macmillan, 2008), pp. 135–50.

Vatter, Miguel, 'Foucault and Hayek: Republican Law and Liberal Civil Society', in Vanessa Lemm and Miguel Vatter (eds), *The Government of Life: Foucault, Biopolitics, and Neoliberalism* (New York: Fordham University Press, 2014), pp. 163–84.

Vaughan-Williams, Nick, 'The Generalised Bio-Political Border? Reconceptualisting the Limits of Sovereign Power', *Review of International Studies* 35 (2009), pp. 729–49.

Visker, Rudi, 'The Inhuman Core of Human Dignity: Levinas and Beyond', *Levinas Studies* 9 (2014), pp. 1–21.

Wainer, Devorah, 'Beyond the Wire: Levinas vis-à-vis Villawood' (doctoral thesis, University of Technology, Sydney, 2010).

Waldron, Jeremy, *The Right to Private Property* (Oxford: Clarendon, 1988).

Waldron, Jeremy, 'Theoretical Foundations of Liberalism', *The Philosophical Quarterly* 37 no. 147 (1987), pp. 127–50.

Weyrauch, Walter O., and Maureen Anne Bell, 'Autonomous Lawmaking: The Case of the "Gypsies"', *Yale Law Journal* 103 (1993), pp. 323–99.

Wistrich, Andrew J., 'The Evolving Temporality of Lawmaking', *Connecticut Law Review* 44 no. 3 (2012), pp. 737–826.

Wolcher, Louis, 'Ethics, Justice, and Suffering in the Thought of Levinas: The Problem of the Passage', *Law and Critique* 14 no. 1 (2003), pp. 93–116.

Žižek, Slavoj, *Did Somebody Say Totalitarianism? Five Interventions in the Mis(Use) of a Notion* (London: Verso, 2001).

Žižek, Slavoj, 'Neighbors and Other Monsters: A Plea for Ethical Violence', in Slavoj Žižek, Eric L. Santner and Kenneth Reinhard, *The Neighbor: Three Inquiries in Political Theology* (Chicago and London: University of Chicago Press, 2005), pp. 134–90.

Index